MW01643749

# *Great Thoughts From the Upper Room*

CLARION CLASSICS

Great Thoughts From the Upper Room
With Christ in the School of Prayer
Robert Murray McCheyne: A Biography
The Imitation of Christ

# Great Thoughts From the Upper Room

F. B. Meyer

ZONDERVAN PUBLISHING HOUSE
OF THE ZONDERVAN CORPORATION
GRAND RAPIDS, MICHIGAN 49506

*Great Thoughts From the Upper Room*


The chapters in this book were formerly chapters 37-58 in F. B. Meyer's *A Commentary on the Gospel of John.*

Designed by Ann Cherryman



**Library of Congress Cataloging in Publication Data**
Meyer, F. B. (Frederick Brotherton), 1847-1929.
Great thoughts from the upper room.

(Clarion classics)
"The chapters in this book were formerly chapters 37-58 in F. B. Meyer's A commentary on the Gospel of John"—T.p. verso.
1. Bible. N.T. John—Meditations. I. Title.
II. Series.
BS2615.4.M48 1983 226'.506 83-10315
ISBN 0-310-44601-5

*Printed in the United States of America*

83 84 85 86 87 88 — 10 9 8 7 6 5 4 3 2 1

# Contents

# *F. B. Meyer*

Frederick Brotherton Meyer was one of a great galaxy of Christian preachers who graced the late Victorian through the early Georgian era, along with C. H. Spurgeon, D. L. Moody, J. H. Jowett, G. Campbell Morgan, and T. DeWitt Talmadge. Born on April 8, 1847, he lived a life of ceaseless external activity while being filled with inner peace. It was difficult for others to keep up with him. Once, while on a speaking tour in Wales, he told his exhausted companion, Dr. Charles Brown, that his motto was, "Give every flying minute/ Something to keep in store." He died on March 28, 1929 after a short illness. Although one of the outstanding preachers of his age, Meyer's assessment of himself was modest in the extreme, and perhaps therein lies his true greatness:

"I am only an ordinary man and I have no special gifts," he said. "I am no orator, no scholar, no profound thinker. If I have done anything for Christ and my generation, it is because I have given myself entirely to Christ Jesus, and then tried to do whatever He wanted me to do." This echoed his daily prayer from the time he was five years old, "Put Thy Holy Spirit in me to make my heart good, like Jesus Christ was."

During the course of his many years of ministry, Meyer was variously pastor of Melbourne Hall, Leicester; Christ Church, Westminster Bridge Road, London; and Regent's Park Chapel, London. He was renowned for his warm, pastoral messages that settled the anxious hearts of many troubled listener. He would write out his sermons, labor over the turns of phrase and cadence, commit them wholly to memory, and deliver them as an orator would. Admirable as that was, it stood in the way of Meyer's expressing his deepest feelings spontaneously to his congregation, so he abandoned it for a less formal, but more direct approach. The result was a breaking through the stiffness that characterized that age, to a warm speaking style that went from heart to heart. This resulted in changed lives, rather than merely pleased intellects.

A restlessness characterized Meyer's spiritual life until he was in his forties. His almost incessant activity trying to help the underprivileged, the widows, the alcoholics, the derelicts, and the dispossessed often brought great anxiety to his soul and caused him to ask where the answer might lie to genuine peace of soul. Meyer drew back the veil from his own deepest experiences and told of two almost visionary occurrences that (in his words) reached the "high-water mark." They were to guide him for the rest of his life. The first happened in Melbourne Hall, described by Meyer in this fashion:

> "The visit of Messrs. Stanley Smith and Studd to Melbourne Hall will always mark an epoch in my own life. Before then my Christian life was spasmodic and fitful; now flaming up with enthusiasm, and then pacing weariedly over leagues of grey ashes and cold cinders. I saw that these young men had something which I had not, but which was within them a constant source of rest and strength and joy. And never shall I forget a scene at 7 a.m. in the grey November morning, as daylight was flickering into the bedroom, paling the guttered candles which from a very early hour had been lighting up the page of Scripture and revealing the figures of the devoted Bible students, who wore the old cricketing or boating costume of earlier days, to render them less sensible of the raw, damp climate. The talk we held then was one of the most formative influences of my life. Why should I not do what they had done? Why should I not yield my whole nature to God, working out day by day that which He would will and work within? Why should I not be a vessel though only of earthenware, meet for the Master's use, because purged and sanctified?
>
> "There was nothing new in what they told me. They said, that 'A man must not only believe in Christ for final

salvation, but must trust Him for victory over every sin, and for deliverance from every care.' They said, that 'The Lord Jesus was willing to abide in the heart which was wholly yielded up to Him.' They said, that 'If there were some things in our lives that made it difficult for us to surrender our whole nature to Christ, yet if we were willing to be made willing to surrender them, He would make us not only willing but glad.' They said, that 'Directly we give or attempt to give ourselves to Him, He takes us.' All this was simple enough. I could have said it myself. But they urged me to take the definite step; and I shall be for ever thankful that they did. And if in a distant country they should read this page, let them be encouraged to learn that one heart at least has been touched with new fire, and that one voice is raised in prayer for their increase in the knowledge and love of Him Who has become more real to the suppliant, because of their brotherly words.

"Very memorable was the night when I came to close quarters with God. The Angel that wrestled with Jacob found me, eager to make me a Prince. There were things in my heart and life which I felt were questionable, if not worse; I knew that God had a controversy with respect to them; I saw that my very dislike to probe or touch them was a clear indication that there was mischief lurking beneath. It is the diseased joint that shrinks from the touch and tender eye that shudders at the light. At the same time I did not feel willing to give these things up. It was a long struggle. At last I said feebly, 'Lord, I am willing to be made Willing; I am desirous that Thy will should be done in me and through me, as thoroughly as it is done in Heaven; come and take me and break me and make me.' That was the hour of crisis, and when it had passed I felt able at once to add, 'And now I give myself to thee: body, soul and spirit; in sorrow or in joy; in the dark or in the light; in life or in death, to be Thine only, wholly and for ever. Make the most of me that can be made for Thy glory.' No rapture or rush of joy came to assure me that the gift was accepted. I left the place with almost a heavy heart. I simply assured myself that He must have taken that which I had given, and at the moment of my giving it. And to that belief I clung in all the days that followed, constantly repeating to myself the words, 'I am His.' And thus at last the joy and rest entered and victory and freedom from burdening care and I found that He was moulding my will and making it easy to do what I had thought impossible; and I felt that He was leading me into the paths of righteousness for His name's sake, but so gently as to be almost imperceptible to my weak sight."

The second notable experience that Meyer had was in Keswisch, in 1887, when he retreated to the hills to find what was missing in his own life. He recounts it this way:

Before I first spoke on the platform I had my own deeper experience, on a memorable night when I left the little town with its dazzling lamps, and climbed the neighbouring hill. As I write the summer night is again casting its spell on me. The light clouds veil the stars and pass. The breath of the mountains leads me to yearn for a fresh intake of God's Spirit. May we not count on the Anointing Spirit to grant us a fresh infilling when we are led to seek it? May we not dare to believe that we have received, even when there is no answering emotion? Do we not receive by faith? These were the questions which a few of us had debated far into the night, at a prayer meeting convened at which a number of men were agonizing for the Spirit.

"I was too tired to agonize, so I left that prayer meeting and as I walked I said, 'My Father, if there is one soul more than another within the circle of these hills that needs the gift of Pentecost it is I; I want the Holy Spirit but I do not know how to receive Him and I am too weary to think, or feel, or pray intensely.' Then a Voice said to me, 'As you took forgiveness from the hand of the dying Christ, take the Holy Ghost from the hand of the living Christ, and reckon that the gift is thine by a faith that is utterly indifferent to the presence or absence of resultant joy. According to thy faith so shall it be unto thee.'

So I turned to Christ and said, 'Lord, as I breathe in this whiff of warm night air, so I breathe into every part of me Thy blessed Spirit.' I felt no hand laid on my head, there was no lambent flame, there was no rushing sound from heaven: but by faith, without emotion, without excitement, I took, and took for the first time, and I have kept on taking ever since.

"I turned to leave the mountain side, and as I went down the tempter said I had nothing, that it was all imagination, but I answered, 'Though I do not feel it, I reckon that God is faithful.'"

Not everyone will come to a deeper understanding of God in the same way, and Meyer knew this. It was not the experience of God that was important, but God Himself. After he had written up his earlier experience in tract form, he was asked to elaborate on it for some felt it had ultimate value in itself; he refused, saying, "No, no. You cannot live on an experience." Experiences are like lamps for the road: they offer light, but we must walk on, leaving the light behind us if we are to make any progress.

Meyer was the author of more than seventy volumes, many of which have been translated into other languages. He also wrote about three dozen booklets that had a combined printing of more than two million copies. Most of his books deal with biblical and devotional themes. He would often combine both by taking the life of a biblical saint, showing how his life can become a pattern for our own.

*Great Thoughts From the Upper Room* is one of Meyer's expository works, some of the others being: *Christ in Isaiah; Tried by Fire—on the Epistles of Peter; The Epistle to the Philippians; The Book of Exodus; Devotional Commentary on the Psalms. Great Thoughts From the Upper Room* was originally the chapters consisting of our Lord's discourse to His disciples in the Upper Room (John 13-17) taken from Meyer's commentary on the Gospel of John.

Meyer wants us to understand that the nearness of God is our strength. He is present to us in Himself, in Christ, in the Holy Spirit, and in the needs of others that call us out of ourselves into a life of commitment and service. The deeper we go into true life, the deeper we get into God, and there, ultimate blessedness is found.

*Walter Elwell*
Wheaton College
Wheaton, Illinois

# 1 The Laver in the Life of Jesus

*He poureth water into a basin, and began to wash the disciples' feet and to wipe them with the towel wherewith he was girded.*

*John 13:5*

In the court of the temple there were two objects that arrested the eye of the entering worshiper—the brazen altar, and the laver. The latter was always kept full of pure, fresh water, for the constant washings enjoined by the Levitical code. Before the priests were consecrated for their holy work, and attired in the robes of the sacred office, they washed there (Exod. 29:4). Before they entered the Holy Place in their ordinary ministry, and before Aaron, on the great Day of Atonement, proceeded to the Most Holy Place, with blood, not his own, it was needful to conform to the prescribed ablutions. "He shall wash his flesh in water" (Lev. 16:4).

First, then, the laver, and then the Holy Place; the order is irreversible, and the teaching of the types is as exact as mathematics. Therefore, when the writer of the Epistle to the Hebrews invites us to draw near, and make our abode in the Most Holy Place, he carefully obeys the divine order, and bids us "draw near with a true heart in full assurance of faith, having our hearts sprinkled from an evil conscience, and our bodies washed with pure water" (10:22).

In this scene (John 13:1-14), on the eve of our Lord's betrayal, we find the spiritual counterpart of the laver, and in the following chapters we stand in the Presence Chamber.

**The Circumstance That Led to This Act of Love** In order to fully understand this touching incident, it is necessary to remember the circumstances out of which it sprang. On the way from Bethany to the Upper Room in which the Supper had been prepared, and on entering the room, our Lord must have been deeply absorbed in the momentous events in which He was to be the central figure; but He was not unmindful of a contention that had engaged His disciples, for they had been disputing one with another as to who of them should be the greatest. The proud spirit of the flesh, which so often cursed the little group, broke out in this awful hour with renewed energy; it was as though the prince of this world would inflict a parting blow on his great Antagonist, through those whom He loved best. It was as if Satan said, "See the results of Your tears and teaching, of Your prayers and pleadings; the love that You have so often taught is but a passing sentiment that has never rooted itself in the soil of these wayward hearts. It is a plant too rare and exotic for the climate of earth. Take it back with You to Your own home if You will, but seek not to achieve the impossible."

It was heartrending that this exhibition of pride should take place just at this juncture. These were the men who had been with Him in His temptations, who had had the benefit of His most careful instructions, who had been exposed to the full influence of His personal character; and yet, notwithstanding all, the rock-bed of pride, that had cast the angels down from heaven, that had led to the fall of man, obtruded itself. This occasion in which it manifested itself was very inopportune; already the look of Calvary was on the Savior's face, and the sword was entering His heart. Surely, they must have been aware that the shadow of the great eclipse was already passing over the face of their Sun. But even this did not avail to restrain the manifestation of their pride. Heedless of three years of example and teaching; unrestrained by the symptoms of our Lord's sorrow; unchecked by the memory of happy and familiar intercourse, which should have bound them forever in a united brotherhood, they wrangled with high voices and hot faces, with the flashing eye and clenched fist of the Oriental, as to who should be first.

And if pride asserted itself after *such* education, and under *such* circumstances, let us be sure that it is not far away from any one of us. We do not now contend in so many words for the chief places; courtesy, politeness, fear of losing the respect of others, restrain us. But our resentment to the fancied slight, or the assumption by another of work that we thought our own; our sense of hurtness when we are put aside; our jealousy and envy; our detracting speeches, and subtle insinuations of low motive, all show how much of this loveless spirit rankles in our hearts. We have been planted in the soil of this world, and we betray its flavor; we have come of a proud stick, and we betray our heredity.

**Love's Sensitiveness to Sin on the Part of Its Beloved**

Consider these epithets of the love of Christ:

*It was unusually tender.* When the hour of departure approaches, though slight reference is made to it, love lives with the sound of the departing wheels or the scream of the engine always in its ear; and there is given a tenderness to the tone, a delicacy to the touch, a thoughtfulness for the heartache of those from whom it is to be parted, which are of inexpressible beauty. All that was present with Christ. He was eating that Supper with them before He suffered. He knew that He would soon depart out of this world to the Father. His ear was especially on the alert, His nature keenly alive, His heart thrilling with unusual tenderness, as the sands slowly ran out from the hourglass.

*It was supreme love.* "Having loved his own which were in the world, he loved them unto the end" (John 13:1). These last words have been thought to refer to the end of life, but it surely would be superfluous to tell us that the strong waters of death could not quench the love of the Son of Man. When once He loves, He loves always. It is needless to tell us that the divine heart that has enshrined a soul will not forsake it; that the name of the beloved is never erased from the palms of the hands; that the covenant is not forgotten though eternity elapse. Of course Christ loves to the end, even though that end reaches to endlessness. We do not need to be assured that the Immortal Lover, who has once taken us into union with Himself, can never loose His hold. Therefore it is better to adopt the alternative suggested by some, "He loved them to the uttermost." There was nothing to be desired. Nothing was needed to fill out the ideal of perfect love. Not a stitch was required for the needlework of wrought gold; not a touch demanded for the perfectly achieved picture; not a throb added to the strong pulse of affection with which He regarded His own.

It is wonderful that He should have loved such men like this. As we pass them under review at this time of their life, they seem a collection of nobodies—with the exception perhaps of John and Peter. But they were His own, there was a special relationship between Him and them. They had belonged to the Father, and He had given them to the Son as His special due and belonging. "Thine they were, and thou gavest them me" (John 17:6). Dare we, in this meaning, to apply to Christ that sense of proprietorship that makes a bit of moorland waste, a few yards of garden ground, dear to the freeholder?

> Breathes there the man with soul so dead,
> Who never to himself hath said,
> This is my own . . . ?"

It was because these men were Christ's *own,* that the full passion of His heart set in toward them, and He loved them to the utmost; that is, the tides filled the capacity of the ocean bed of possibility.

*It was bathed in the sense of His divine origin and mission.* The curtain was waxing very thin. It was a moment of vision. There had swept across His soul a realization of the full meaning of His approaching triumph. He looked back, and was hardly conscious of the manger where the horned oxen fed, of the lowly birth, of the obscure years, in the sublime conception that He had come forth from God. He looked forward, and was hardly conscious of the cross, the nail, the crown of thorns, and the spear, because of the sublime consciousness that He was stepping back, to go to Him with whom He realized His identity. He looked on through the coming weeks, and knew that the Father had given all things into His hands. What the devil had offered as the price of obeisance to Himself, that the Father was about to give Him—no, had already given Him—as the price of his self-emptying. And if for a moment He stooped, as we shall see He did, to the form of a servant, it was not because of any failure to recognize his high dignity and mission, but with the sense of Godhead alive on his soul.

The love that went out toward this little group of men had deity in it. It was the love of the throne, of the glory He had with the Father before the worlds were, of that which now fills the bosom of His ascended and glorified nature.

*He was aware of the task to which He was abandoning these men.* He knew that as He was the High Priest over the house of God, they were its priests. He knew that cleansing was necessary before they could receive the anointing of the Holy Ghost. He knew that the great work of carrying forward His gospel was to be delegated to their hands. He knew that they were to carry the sacred vessels of the gospel, which must not be blurred or fouled by contact with human pride or uncleanness. He knew that the very mysteries of Gethsemane and Calvary would be inexplicable, and that none might stand on that holy hill, save those who had clean hands and a pure heart. And because of all this, He turned to them, by symbol and metaphor, to impress upon their heart and memory the necessity of participating in the cleansing of which the laver is the type.

The highest love is always quickest to detect the failures and inconsistencies of the beloved. Just because of its intensity, it can be content with nothing less than the best, because the best means the most blessed; and it desires that the object of its thought should be most blessed forever. It is a mistake to think that green-eyed jealousy is quickest to detect the spots on the sun, the freckles on the face, and the jarring discords in the music of the life; love is quicker, more microscopic, more exacting that the ideal should be achieved. Envy is content to indicate the fault, and leave it; but love detects, and waits and holds its peace until the fitting opportunity arrives, and then sets itself to remove, with its own tenderest ministry, the defect that had spoiled the completeness and beauty of its object.

Perhaps there had never been a moment in the human consciousness of our Lord, when, side by side with this intense love for His own, there had been so vivid a sense of oneness with His Father, of His unity with the source of Infinite Purity and Blessedness. We might have supposed that this would have alienated Him from His poor friends, but in this our thoughts are not as His. Just because of His awesome holiness, He was quick to perceive the unholiness of His friends, and could not endure it, and essayed to rid them of it. Just because of His divine goodness, He could detect the possibilities of goodness in them, and be patient enough to give it culturing care.

The most perfect musician may be most tortured by incompetence; but he will be most likely to detect true merit, and give time to its training. "The most powerfull magnet will pick out, in the powdered dust of the ironstone, fine particles of metal that a second- or third-rate magnet would fail to draw to itself." Do not dread the awesome holiness of Jesus; it is your hope. He will never be content until He has made you like Himself; and side by side with His holiness, never fail to remember His gentle, tender love.

**The Divine Humility, That Copes With Human Sin.**

"He riseth from supper, and laid aside his garments; and took a towel, and girded himself." This is what the apostle calls taking upon Himself the form of a servant. The charm of the scene is its absolute simplicity. You cannot imagine Christ posturing to the ages. There was no aiming at effect, no thought of the beauty or humility of the act, as there is when the Pope yearly washes the feet of twelve beggars, from a golden basin, wiping them with a towel of rarest fabric! Christ did not act for show or pretense, but with an absolutely single purpose of fulfilling a needed office. And in this He set forth the spirit of our redemption.

*This is the key to the Incarnation.* With slight alteration the words will read truly of that supreme act. He rose from the throne; laid aside the garments of light that He had worn as His vesture; took up the poor towel of humanity, and wrapped it about His glorious Person; poured His own blood into the basin of the cross; and set Himself to wash away the foul stains of human depravity and guilt.

As pride was the source of human sin, Christ must needs provide an antidote in His absolute humility—a humility that could not grow beneath these skies, but must be brought from the world where the lowliest are the greatest, and the most childlike reign as kings.

*This is the key to every act of daily cleansing.* We have been washed—once, definitely and irrevocably, we have been bathed in the crimson tide that flows from Calvary; but we need a daily cleansing. Our feet become soiled with the dust of life's highways; our hands grimy, as our linen beneath the rain of filth in a great city; our lips—as the white doorstep of the house—are fouled by the incessant throng of idle, unseemly, and fretful words; our hearts cannot keep unsoiled the stainless robes with which we pass from the closet at morning prime. Constantly we need to return to the laver to be washed. But do we always realize how much each act of confession on our part involves from Christ on His? Whatever important work He may at that moment have on hand; whatever directions He may be giving to the loftiest angels for the fulfillment of His purposes; however pressing the concerns of the church or the universe on His broad shoulders—He must needs turn from all these to do a work He will not delegate. Again He stoops from the throne, and girds Himself with a towel; and, in all lowliness, endeavors to remove from you and me the stain which His love dare not pass over. He never loses the print of the nails; He never forgets Calvary and the blood; He never spends one hour without stooping to do the most menial work of cleansing filthy souls. And it is because of this humility He sits on the throne and wields the scepter over hearts and worlds.

*This is the key to our ministry to each other.* I have often thought that we do not often enough wash one another's feet. We are conscious of the imperfections that mar the characters of those around us. We are content to note, criticize, and learn them. We dare not attempt to remove them. This failure arises partly because we do not love with a love like Christ's—a love that will brave resentment, annoyance, rebuke, in its quest—and partly because we are not willing to stoop low enough.

None can remove the mote of another, so long as the beam is left in the eye, and the sin unjudged in the life. None can cleanse the stain, who is not willing to take the form of a servant, and go down with bare knees on the floor. None is able to restore those who are overtaken in a fault, who does not count himself the chief of sinners and the least of saints.

We need more of this lowly, loving spirit: not so sensitive to wrong and evil as they affect us, as anxious for the stain they leave on the offender. It is of comparatively small consequence how much we suffer; it is of much importance that none of Christ's disciples should be allowed to go on for a moment longer, with unconfessed and unjudged wrongs clouding his peace, and hindering the testimony that he might give. Let us therefore watch for each other's souls: let us consider one another to provoke to love and good works; let us in all sincerity do as Christ has done, washing each other's feet in all humility and tender love. But this spirit is impossible save through fellowship with the Lamb of God, and the reception of His holy, humble nature into the inmost heart, by the Holy Spirit.

# 2 Thrice Bidden to Love

*A new commandment I give unto you, That ye love one another; as I have loved you, that ye also love one another.*
*John 13:34*

Anocræon complains that when they asked him to sing of heroic deeds, he could only sing of love. But the love with which he fills his sonnets will bear as much comparison with that of which Jesus spoke in His last discourse, as the flaring oil of a country fair with the burning of the heavenly constellations. Even the love that binds young hearts is too selfish and exclusive to set forth that pure ray that shone from the heart of the Son of Man, and shines, and will shine. What word shall we use to describe it?

*Charity?* The disposition denoted by this great word does not fulfill the measure of the love of Christ. It is cold and severe. It can be organized. It casts its dole to the beggar and turns away, content to have relieved the sentiment of pity. By being employed for one manifestation of love, charity is too limited and restricted in its significance to become an adequate expression of the divine love that brought Jesus from the throne, and should inspire us to lay down our lives for the brethren.

*Philanthropy?* This is a great word, "the love of man." And yet the philanthropist is too often content with the general patronage of good works, the elaboration of schemes, the management of committees to do much personal work for the amelioration of the world. The word is altogether too distant, too deficient in the personal element, too extensive in its significance. It will not serve to represent the divine compassion with which the heart of Christ was, at the moment of speaking, in tumult.

*Complacency?* No; for this is the emotion excited by the contemplation of merit and virtue, which turns away from sin and deformity; and the sentiment denoted by our Master's words is one that is not brought into existence by virtue, nor extinguished by demerit and vice.

Since all these words fail, we are driven to speak of love, as Christ used the word, as being the essence of the divine nature; for God is Love. It is the indwelling of God in the soul. It is the transmitting through our lives of that which we have received in fellowship with the uncreated glory of the divine Being. That which was in the beginning between the Father and the Son; that which constrained our Emmanuel to sojourn in this world of sin; that which inspired His sacrifice; that which dwells perennially in His heart, vanquishing time and distance; which overflows all expressions, and defies definition—is the love of which these words speak, and which we are commanded to entertain toward each other.

*It is a commandment.* "These things I command you." "This is his commandment, That we should believe on the name of his Son Jesus Christ, and love one another, as he gave us commandment" (1 John 3:23). Obviously, then, obedience must be possible. Christ had gauged our nature not only as Creator, but by personal experience. He knew what was in man. The possibilities of our nature were well within His cognizance; therefore it must be possible for us to love one another qualitatively, if not quantitatively, as He has loved us. Do not sit down before this great command and say it is impossible; that would throw discredit on Him who spoke it. Dare to believe that no word of His is vain. He detects the eminence of attainment that is possible for us all to reach: let us surrender ourselves to Him, that He may fulfill in us His ideal, and make us experts in the science of love.

*It is a new commandment.* Archbishop Ussher on a memorable occasion called it the eleventh commandment. It is recorded that having heard of the simplicity and beauty of the ordering of Rutherford's home, he resolved to visit it for himself. One Saturday night he arrived alone at the manse, and asked for entertainment over the next day. A simple but hearty welcome was accorded him; and after partaking of the frugal fare, he was invited to join the household in religious exercises that ushered in the Lord's Day.

"How many commandments are there?" the master asked his guest, wholly unaware who he was.

"Eleven," was the astonishing reply; at which the very servants were scandalized, regarding the newcomer as a prodigy of ignorance. But the man of God perceived the rare light of character and insight that gleamed beneath the answer, and asked for a private interview. This issued in the invitation to preach on the following day. To the amazement of the household, so scandalized on the previous night, the stranger appeared in the master's pulpit, and announced as his text the words on which we are meditating, adding, "This may be described as the eleventh commandment."

*Obedience to this fulfills the rest.* Love is the fulfilling of the law. Do we need to be told to have no other gods but God, to forbear taking His name in vain, and to devote one day in seven to the cultivation of a closer relationship with Him, if we love Him with all our soul and mind and strength? Do we need to be warned against killing our neighbor, stealing his goods, or bearing false witness against his character, if we love Him as ourselves? Only let a man be filled with this divine disposition which is the unique characteristic of God; let him be filled with the spirit of love; let him be perfected in love: and, almost unconsciously, he will not only be kept from infringing the prohibitions of the law of Sinai, but will be inspired to fulfill the requirements of the Mount of Beatitudes. Love, and do as you like. You will like to do only what God would like you to do.

*There is a very important purpose to be realized in obeying this command.* "By this shall all men know that ye are my disciples, if ye have love one to another." Every church claims to be the true representative of Christ—the Eastern, because it occupies the lands where Christianity was cradled; the Roman Catholic, because it professes to be able to trace its orders to the apostles. But, amid the hubbub of rival claims, the world, unconvinced, still awaits the emergence of the true

Bride of the Lamb. The one note of the true church is love. When once men of different nationalities and countries behold its manifestation, they do not hesitate to acknowledge the presence of God, and to admit that those who are animated by perfect love to Him and to one another constitute a unique organization that cannot have originated in the will or intellect of man but, like the New Jerusalem, must have come out of heaven from God. So sublime, so transcendent, so unearthly is love, that its presence is significant of the handiwork of God as the fire that burned in the bush indicated that the "I AM" was there.

Love is the supreme test, not only of the church, but also of the individual. It has been the mistake of every age to make faith rather than love the test of Christianity—"Tell me how much a man believes, and I shall know how good a Christian he is!" The whole endeavor of the mediæval church was to reduce the followers of Christ to a uniformity of belief. And in our own time, a man is permitted by consent to be of a grasping disposition, imperious in temper, uncharitable in speech, without losing position in the church, so long as he assents to all the clauses of an orthodox creed.

With Christ, however, love is all-important. A man may have faith enough to remove mountains, but if he have not love, he is nothing, and lighter than vanity in the estimation of heaven. Faith ranks with hope and love, but it is destined to pass as the blossoms of spring before the fruit of autumn, while love shall abide for evermore. A man may have a very inadequate creed; like the woman of old, he may think there is virtue in a garment; like Thomas, he may find it impossible to attain the exuberant confidence of his brethren; but if he loves Christ enough to be prepared to die for Him, if through the narrow aperture of a very limited faith love enough has entered his soul from the source of love, Christ will entrust him with the tending of His sheep and lambs, and call him into the secret place. Of course, the more full-orbed and intelligent our faith, the quicker and more intense will be our love. But faith, after all, is but the hand that takes, while love is the fellowship of kindred hearts that flash each on the other the enkindling gleam.

If you do not love, though you count yourself illumined with the light of perfect knowledge, you are in the dark. "He that . . . hateth his brother, is in darkness even until now" (1 John 2:9).

If you do not love, you are dead. "He that loveth not . . . abideth in death" (1 John 3:14). The light sparkle of intellectual or emotional life may illumine your words and fascinate your immediate circle of friends, but there will be no life toward God. *Love* is the perfect tense of *live*. Whoso does not love does not live, in the deepest sense. There are capacities for richer existence that never unfold until love stands at the portal and sounds his challenge, and summons the sleeper to awake and arise.

If you do not love, you are under the thrall of the devil, into whose dark nature love never comes. "In this the children of God are manifest, and the children of the devil. . . . Cain was of that wicked one, and slew his brother" (1 John 3:10, 12).

"As I have loved you." Life is one long education to know the love of God. "We have known and believed the love that God hath to us," is the reflection of an old man reviewing the past. Each stage of life, each phase of experience, is intended to give us a deeper insight into the love wherewith we are loved; and as each discovery breaks upon our glad vision, we are bidden to exemplify it to others. Does Jesus forgive to the seventy-seventh time? We must forgive in the same measure. Does Jesus forget as well as forgive? We, too, must forget after the same fashion. Does Jesus seek after the erring, and endeavor to induce the temper of mind that will crave forgiveness? We also must seek the man who has transgressed against us, endeavoring to lead him to a better mind. The Christian knows no law or limit but that imposed by these significant words, spoken on the eve of Christ's sacrifice: "As I have loved you."

Thus all life gives opportunities for the practice of this celestial temper and disposition. It has been said that talent develops in solitude, while character is made in the strain of life. Be it so. Then the character of loving may be made stronger by every association we have with others. Each contact with men, women, and children may give us an opportunity of loving with a little more of the strength, purity, and sweetness of the love of Christ. The busiest life can find time for the cultivation of this spirit. That which is spent in a crowd will even have greater opportunities than the one that is limited to solitude. The distractions and engagements that threaten to break up our lives into a number of inconsiderable fragments may thus conduce to a higher unity than could be gained by following one occupation, or concentrating ourselves on one object.

Let us gird up the loins of our minds, and resolve to seek a baptism of love from the Holy Spirit, that we may be perfected in love; that we may love God first, and all else in Him; ascending from our failures to a more complete conformity to the love wherewith He has loved us; embracing the sinful and erring in the compass of our compassion, as we embrace the divine and eternal in the compass of our adoration and devotion.

# 3 *Heaven Delayed But Guaranteed*

*Simon Peter said unto him, Lord, whither goest thou? Jesus answered him, Whither I go, thou canst not follow me now; but thou shalt follow me afterwards.*

*John 13:36*

These chapters are holy ground. The last words of our Lord, spoken in the seclusion of the death-chamber to the tear-stained group gathered around, are not for all the world, and are recorded only for those whose love makes them able to appreciate. And what are these words that now begin to flow from the Master's lips, but His last to His own. They were held back so long as Judas was there. There was a repression caused by his presence that hindered the interchange of confidence; but, when he was gone, love hastened to her secret stores, and drew forth her choicest, rarest viands to share them, that they might be in after days a strength and solace.

This marvelous discourse, which begins in 13:31, continues through chapters 14, 15, 16, and closes in the sublime prayer of chapter 17. Better that all the literature of the world should have shared the fate of the Alexandrian library, than that these precious words should have been lost amid the fret of the ages.

The Lord begins His discourse by speaking of His speedy departure. "Little chidren," He said, using a term that indicated that He felt toward them a parental tenderness, and spoke as a dying father might have done to the helpless babes that gathered around his bed, "I am to be with you for a very little time longer; the sand has nearly run out in the hourglass. I know you will seek Me; your love will make you yearn to be with Me where I am, to continue the blessed intimacy, the ties that within the last few weeks have been drawn so much closer; but it will not be possible. As I said to the Jews, so I must say to you, where I go, ye cannot come." He then proceeds to give them a new commandment of love, as though He said: "The *cannot* that prevents you following Me now is due to a lack of perfect love on your part, as well as for other reasons; it is necessary, therefore, that you wait to acquire it, before you can be with Me where I am."

Simon Peter hardly hears Him uttering these last words; he is pondering too deeply what he has just heard, and calls the Master back to that announcement, as though He had passed it with too light a tread: "Going away! Lord, where are You going?" To that question our Lord might have given a direct answer: "Heaven! The Father's bosom! The New Jerusalem! The City of God!" Any of these would have been sufficient; but instead, He says in effect: "It is a matter of comparative indifference where I go; I have no wish to feed curiosity with descriptions of things in the heavens, which you could not understand. The main point for you, in this brief life, is to become assimilated to Me in humility, devotion, likeness, and character, that you may be able to be My companion and friend in those new paths on which I am entering, as you have been in those which I am now leaving. "Whither I go, thou canst not follow me now; but thou shalt follow me afterwards.' "

The words staggered Peter; he could not understand what Christ meant; he could not see how much had to be done before he could share in Christ's coming glory. He made the same mistake as James and John had made before, and wanted the throne, without perceiving that it was conditioned on fellowship in the cup and the baptism into death. With deep emotion he persisted in his inquiries: "Why cannot I follow You now? There is no place on earth to which I would not go with You. Have I not already left all to follow You? Have I not been with You on the Transfiguration Mount, as well as in Your journeyings? There is but one experience through which I have not passed with You, and that is death; but if that stands next in Your life-plan, I will lay down my life for Your sake. Anything to be with You."

How little Peter knew himself! How much better did Christ know him. "What! do you profess yourself willing to die with Me? Truly, truly, I say to you, you will deny Me three times between now and the time the cock crows tomorrow morning." These words silenced Peter for the rest of the evening. He does not appear to have made another remark, but was absorbed in heartbreaking grief; though all the while there rang in his heart those blessed words of hope: "Whither I go, thou canst not follow me now; but thou shalt follow me afterwards"—words which our Lord caught up and expanded for the comfort of them all; for now for the first time they realized that they were about to be parted from Jesus, and were almost beside themselves with grief: "Let not your heart be troubled. . . ."

**The Desire to Be With Christ** This was paramount. These simple men had little thought of heaven as such. If Christ had begun to speak of golden pavement, gates of pearl, and walls of chrysolite, they would have turned from His glowing words with the one inquiry, "Will You be there?" If that question had been answered uncertainly, they would have turned away heartsick, saying: "If You are not there, we have no desire for it; but if You were in the darkest, dreariest spot in the universe, it would be heaven to us."

There were three desires, the strands of which were woven in this one yearning desire and prayer to be with Christ. They wanted His love, His teaching, His leading into full, richer life. And is not this our position also? We want Christ, not hereafter only, but here and now, for these three same reasons.

*We want His love.* There is no love like His—so pure and constant and satisfying. What the sun is to a star, and the ocean to a pool left by the retiring tide, such is the love of Jesus compared with all other love. To have it is superlative blessedness; to miss it is to thirst forever.

*We want His light.* He speaks words that cast light on the mysteries of existence, on the dark problems of life, on the perplexing questions that are perpetually knocking at our doors.

*We want His life.* Fuller and more abundant life is what we crave. It is of life that our veins are lacking. We desire to have the mighty tides of divine life always beating strongly within us, to know the energy, vigor, vitality of God's life in the soul. And we are conscious that this is to be found only in Him.

Therefore we desire to be with Him, to drink deeper into His fellowship, to know Him and the power of His resurrection, to be brought into an abiding from which we shall never recede. We have known Christ after the flesh; we desire to know Him after the Spirit. We have known Him in humiliation; we want to know Him in His glory. We have known Him as the Lamb of the cross; we want to know Him as the divine Man on the throne.

**The Fatal Obstacle to the Immediate Granting of These Desires**

"Thou canst not follow me *now.*" There is thus a difference in His words to His disciples, and those to the Jews. These also were told that they could not follow Him, but the word *now* was omitted. There was no hope held out to them of the great gulf being bridged. This was the *cannot* of moral incompatibility (John 7:34; 8:21); that, of temporary unfitness, which by the grace of God would finally pass away, and the whole of their aspirations be realized.

It is easy to see why Peter was unfit for the deeper realization of Christ in His resurrection. Our Lord had just spoken of being glorified through death. It was as Judas left the chamber, intent on His betrayal, that Jesus said, "Now is the Son of Man glorified!" He saw that the hidden properties of His being could only be unfolded and uttered through death and resurrection. But Peter had little sympathy with this; he might avow his determination to die, but he had never really entered into the meaning of death, and all it might involve.

He could not detect evil. The traitor was beside him; but he had to ask the beloved disciple to elicit from Jesus who it might be by whom the Master would be betrayed.

He was out of sympathy with the Lord's humiliation, so that he chided with Him for stooping to wash his feet; and if he could not understand the significance and necessity of this lowly deed of love, how could he enter into the spirit of that life that was planted in death, and which bore even in resurrection the print of the nails?

He strove with the rest for the primacy. Who should be the greatest was the question that agitated them, as the other evangelists tell us, in that solemn hour. And none that was possessed with that spirit of pride and emulation could be in harmony with that blessed world where the greatest are the lowliest, the highest the least, and the King set on the right hand of power, because he was more capable of humbling Himself than any beside.

But, besides all this, Peter was animated by the strong spirit of self-assertion and determination. On the lake shore he had always been able to get to the front by his stronger voice, and broader shoulders, and more vehement manner. Why should he not do the same now? Why could he not keep pace with Christ even through the dark valley, and accompany Him through unknown worlds?

It cannot be, said Christ; you are too strong in your carnal strength, too self-reliant, too confident. It is not possible for you to be with Me in the life that springs from death, and to which death is the door, until you have deeply drunk into the spirit of My death. You are too strong to follow Me when I descend to the lowest on My way to the highest; I must take for my companion now a forgiven malefactor; but I will some day come for you, and receive you to Myself.

So Peter had to be broken on the wheel of a servant girls' question, and humbled to the dust. In those bitter hours he was thoroughly emptied of his old proud, self-reliant, vainglorious spirit, and became as a little child.

This must be our path also. We must descend with Christ, if we would ascend to sit at His side. We must submit to the laying of our pride in the very dust. We must accept humiliations and mortifications, the humblings of perpetual failure and shortcoming, the friction and fret of infirmity and pain; and when we have come to an end of ourselves, we shall begin to know Christ in a new and deeper fashion. He will pass by and say, "Live!" The spirit of His life will enter into us; the valley of Anchor will become a door of hope, and we shall sing God's glad new song of hope. The ideal that had long haunted us—in our blood, but unable to express itself—will burst into a perfect flower of exquisite scent and hue.

**The Certainty of the Ultimate Gratification of Every Desire God Has Implanted**

This is an absolute certainty, that God inserts no desire or craving in our nature, for which there is no appropriate gratification. The birds do not seek for food which is not ready for them. The young lions do not ask for prey that is not awaiting them somewhere in the forest glade. Hence the absoluteness of that *shalt*—"Thou *shalt* follow me afterwards." It is as if Jesus said, "I have taught you to love Me, and long after Me; and I will certainly gratify the appetite that I have created."

Pentecost was the divine fulfillment of all those conditions of which we have been speaking. It was not enough that Peter should be an emptied and broken man; he must become also a God-possessed, a Spirit-filled man. Thus only could he be fitted to know Christ after a spiritual sort, and to participate in His resurrection life. It was surely to the advent of the Holy Spirit that our Lord referred in that significant *afterwards.*

We too must seek our share in Pentecost. Do not be content with "Not I"; go on to say, "but Christ." Do not be satisfied with the emptying of the proud self-life; seek the infilling of the Holy Spirit. Do not stop at the cross, or the grave; hasten to the Upper Room, where the disciples are baptized in fire and glory. The Holy Spirit will enable you to abide in Christ, because He will bring Christ to abide in you; and life, through His dear grace, shall be so utterly imbued with fellowship with the blessed Lord, that, whether present or absent, you will live together with Him. It is the person who is really filled with the Spirit of God who can follow Jesus, as Peter afterward did, to prison and to death, who can drink of the cup of which He drank, and be baptized with the baptism with which He was baptized.

"Why should I fear?" asked Basil, of the Roman prefect. "Nothing you have spoken of has any effect upon me. He that hath nothing to lose is not afraid of *confiscation.* You cannot banish me, for the earth is the Lord's. As to *torture,* the first stroke would kill me; and *to kill me is to send me to glory.*"

# 4 *Many Mansions*

*I go to prepare a place for you.*

*John 14:2*

The cure for heart trouble, when the future is full of dread, is faith—faith directed to Jesus; and just such faith as we give God, for He is God. He has shown Himself well worthy of that trust; all His paths toward us have been mercy and truth; and we may therefore safely rest on His disclosures of that blessed life, of which the present is the vestibule. "Let not your heart be troubled," He says; "ye believe in God, believe also in me." Or it might be rendered, "Believe in God, believe also in me."

Let us listen to Him, as He discourses of the Father's house, and its many mansions.

*Heaven is a home.* "My Father's house." What magic power lies in that word! It will draw the wanderer from the ends of the earth; it will nerve the sailor, the soldier, and the explorer with indomitable endurance; it will bring a mist of tears to the eyes of the hardened criminal, and soften the heart of stone. When the bands played "Home, Sweet Home" one night in the trenches of the Crimea, a great sob went through the entire army.

But what constitutes *home?* Not the mere locality or building, but the dear ones who lived there once, but who are scattered never to be reunited, and only one or two of whom are still spared. It was father's house, though it was only a shepherd's hut; he dwelled there, and mother, and our brothers and sisters. And where they dwell, or where wife and child dwell, there is home.

Such is heaven. Think of a large family of noble children, of all ages, from the little child to the young man beginning his business career, returning after long severance to spend a season together in the old ancestral home, situated in its far-reaching grounds, and you can form some idea of what it will be when the whole family of the redeemed gather in the Father's house. All reserve, all shyness, all restraint gone forever. God has given us all the memory of what home was, that we may guess at what awaits us, and be smitten with homesickness. As the German proverb puts it: "Blessed are the homesick, for they shall reach home."

*Heaven is very spacious.* There are "*many* mansions." There is no stint in its accommodation. In the old temple there were spacious courts, long corridors, and innumerable chambers, in which a vast multitude could find a home day and night. The children trooped about and sang around their favorite teacher. The blind and lame sheltered themselves from heat or storm. The priests and Levites in great numbers lived there. And this probably suggested the Master's words.

Heaven, too, will contain immense throngs, without being crowded. It will teem with innumerable hosts of angels, and multitudes of the redeemed which no man can number. Its children will be as the grains of sand that bar the ocean's waves, or the stars that begem the vault of night. But it can easily hold these, and myriads more. Yet there is room! As age after age has poured in its crowds, still the cry has gone forth. There is abundant room! The many mansions are not all tenanted. The orchestra is not full. The complement of priests is not complete.

Do not believe those little souls who would make you believe that heaven is a little place for a select few. If they come to you with that story, tell them to be gone! Tell them that they do not know your Father's heart; tell them that all He does must be worthy of Himself. Jesus shall see of the travail of His soul, and be satisfied.

*Heaven is full of variety.* It is not like one great hall; there are myriads of adjacent rooms, "mansions," which will be fitted up, so to speak, differently. One for the sweet singer, another for the little ones and their teachers, another for the student of the deep mysteries of the kingdom, another for those who may need further instruction in the mysteries of God.

Heaven's life and scenery are as various as the aptitudes and capacities of souls. Its music is not a monotone, but a chorale. It is as a home, where the parents delight to develop the special tastes of their children. This is surely what Jesus meant when He said, "I go to prepare a place for you." He is ever studying our special idiosyncrasies—what we need most, and can do best; and when He has ascertained it, He suits our mansion accordingly.

When a gardener is about to receive some rare exotic, he prepares a place where it will flower and fruit to the best advantage. The naturalist who is notified of the shipment of some new specimen, prepares a habitat as suited as possible to its peculiarities. The mother whose son is returning from sea, prepares a room in which his favorite books and pictures are carefully placed, and all else that her pondering heart can devise to give him pleasure. So, our Lord is anxious to give what is best in us its most suitable nourishment and training. And He will keep our place against our coming. It will not suit another, and will not be given to another.

That all this will be so, is witnessed by the instincts of our hearts; and if it had not been so, He would have told us. That little clause is inimitably beautiful; it seems to teach that where He permits His children to cherish some natural presentiment of the blessed future—its solemn troops and sweet societies; its friendships, recognitions, and fellowships; its holy service and special opportunities—He really assents to our deepest and most cherished thoughts. If it had not been so, He would have told us.

*The charm of heaven will be the Lord's presence.* "Where I am, there ye may be also." We shall see His face, and be forever with Him. What would not men give, if some old manuscripts might turn up with new stories of His wondrous life, new parables as charming as those of the Good Shepherd and the Prodigal Son, new beatitudes, new discourses like that on the Vine. God might have permitted this. But what would it be in comparison with all that lies before! The past has lost much; but the future holds infinitely more. We shall see new Gospels enacted before our eyes, behold Christ as a real visible person in the glory of divine manhood, hear Him speak to us as His friends, and know what He meant when He promised to gird Himself and come forth to serve His servants.

If you are in doubt as to what heaven is like, is it not enough to know that it will be in accord with the nature and presence and choice of Jesus Christ?

After His resurrection, He spent forty days among His disciples, that men might see what the risen life was like. As He was, and is, so shall we be. His body is the pattern in accordance with which ours shall be fashioned. What He was to His friends after His resurrection, we shall be to ours, and they to us. We shall hear the familiar voices and the dear old names, shall resume the dear relationships that death severed, and shall speak again of the holy secrets of our hearts with those who were our twin spirits.

And He will come again, etiher in our death hour, or in His Second Advent, "to receive us" to Himself. If we only could believe this, and trust Him who says it, our hearts would not be troubled, though death itself menaced us; for we should realize that, to be received at the moment of dissolution by the hands of Jesus, into the place on which He has lavished time and thought and love, must be "far better" than the best that earth could offer.

# 5 Jacob's Dream Realized

*Jesus saith unto him, I am the way, the truth, and the life; no man cometh unto the Father, but by me.*

*John 14:6*

We all know more truth than we give ourselves credit for. A moment before the Lord had said, "Whither I go ye know, and the way ye know." Thomas the pessimist—always inclined to look at the dark side of things—directly contradicted Him, saying, "Master, we are absolutely ignorant of the goal to which Thy steps are bending; it is impossible, therefore, for us to know the path that lies through the gloom, and by which Thou art to come to it." This was a strange collision—the Master's "Ye know," and Thomas's "We know not." Which was right?

There is no doubt that Jesus was right, and that they did know. In many a discourse He had given sufficient materials for them to construct a true conception of the Father's house, and the way to it. These materials were lying in some dusty corner of their memory, unused, and Christ knew this. He said, therefore, in effect, "Go back to the teachings I have given you; look carefully through the inventory of your knowledge; let your instincts, illumined by My words, supply the information you need: there are torches in your souls already lighted, that will cast a radiant glow upon the mysteries to the brink of which you have come."

This is true of us all. Christ never conducts us to experiences for which He has not previously prepared us. As the great ocean vessels take in their stores of provisions, day and night, for weeks previous to their sailing; so, by insensible influences, Christ is ever anticipating the strain and stress of coming circumstance, passing on words that are spirit and life, though they may stand in their heavy packing cases in the hold, until we are driven to unpack, examine, and use their contents. At times sorrow is sent for no other purpose than to compel us to take cognizance of our possessions. Many a fabric of manufacture, many an article of diet, many an ingenious process has been suggested in days of scarcity and famine. So, old words and truths come back in our sore need. Christ often speaks to us, as a teacher to a nervous child, saying, "You know quite well, if you would only think a little." More truth is stored in memory than recollection can readily lay hands on.

Thomas persisted in his protestations of ignorance, and so the Lord uttered for his further information the royal sentence, which sums up Christianity in the one simple pronoun "I." It was as if He said to His disciples gathered there, and to His church in all ages, "To have Me, to know Me, to love and obey Me, this is religion; this is the light for every dark hour, the solution for all the mysteries." Christianity is more than a creed, a doctrinal system, a code of rules—it is Christ.

**Christ as the Way**

"I am the Way," said our Lord. The conception of life as a pilgrimage is as old as human speech. On the third page of our Bibles we are told that "Enoch walked with God." The path of the Israelites through the desert was a pilgrim's progress, and the enduring metaphor for our passage from the cross to the Sabbath keeping. Isaiah anticipated the rearing up of a highway that would be called the way of holiness, which would not be trodden by the unclean; no lion should be there, or ravenous beast go up on it; but the ransomed of the Lord would walk there, and go with singing to Zion. But in the furthest flights of inspired imagination, the prophet never dreamt that God Himself would stoop to become the trodden path to Himself, and that the way of holiness was no other than that divine Servant who so often stood before him for portrayal. "*I* am the Way," said Christ.

He fulfills all the conditions of Isaiah's prediction. He saw a highway.

*A highway is for all:* for kings and commoners; for the nobleman daintily picking his way, and the beggar painfully plodding with bare feet. And Jesus is for every man. "Whosoever will, let him come"; let him step out and walk; let him commit himself to Him who comes to our doors that He may conduct us to the pearly gate.

*It was a way of holiness,* where no unclean or leprous person was permitted to travel. Neither can we avail ourselves of the gracious help of Christ, so long as we are harboring what He disapproves, or doing what He forbids.

*It was plain and straight,* so that wayfaring men though fools could not mistake it. And the Master said, that while the wise and prudent might miss His salvation, babes would find it. "Hidden from the wise and prudent, but revealed to babes."

*It afforded perfect immunity from harm.* The wild beasts of the forest might roar around it, but they were kept off that thoroughfare by an invisible and impassable fence. Who is he who can harm us while we follow that which is good? The special divine permission was necessary before Satan could tempt Job, whose heart was perfect with his God.

*It was trodden with song.* And who can describe the waves of joy that sometimes roll in on the believing, loving soul! There is always peace, but sometimes there is joy unspeakable and full of glory. The hands of Jesus shed the oil of gladness on our heads, while the lamentation and regret that haunt the lives of others are abashed, as the specters of the night before the roseate touch of morn.

What further thought did Christ mean to convey, when He said, "I am the Way"? We cannot see the other side of the moon: so the full import of these words, as they touch His wonderful nature, as it lies between Him and His Father, is beyond us; but we may at least study the face they turn toward our lives.

The true value of a way is never realized until we are following it through an unknown country, or groping along it in almost absolute darkness. I remember, during a tour in

Switzerland, on starting for a long day's march, the comfort of the assurance that I had to keep to one road that was clearly defined, and it would inevitably bring me to my destination. How different this from another experience of making my way, as I might, across the hillsides in the direction that I fancied was the right one! All that had to be done in the first instance was to follow the roadway, to *obey* its sinuous windings, to climb the hills where it climbed, to descend the valleys where it descended, to cross the rivers and torrents at the precise point with it. It seemed responsible for me as long as I kept to it. Whenever I thought to better myself by wandering right or left, I found myself landed in some difficulty, and when I returned to the road, it seemed to say, "Why did you leave me? I know that sometimes I am rough and difficult; but I can do better for you than you can for yourself, and indeed I am the only possible way. Obey me, and I will bring you home." It is so that Christ speaks to us.

Each day, as we leave our home, we know that the prepared path lies before us, in the good works that God has prepared for us to walk in. And when we are ignorant of their direction, and are at a loss as to where to place our steps, we have only to concern ourselves with Christ, and almost unconsciously we shall find ourselves making progress in the destined way. Christ is the Way: love Christ, trust Christ, obey Christ, be concerned with Christ, and all else will be added. Christ is the Way. When the heart is wrapped up in Him, it is on the way, and it is making progress, although it never counts the rate or distance, so occupied is it with Him.

"I fear I make no progress," sighs the timid soul.

"But what is Christ to you?"

"Everything."

"Then if He is all in all to you, you are most certainly on God's way; and you are making progress toward your home, albeit it is unconsciously. Be of good cheer. Christ is the Way; remember the ancient pilgrims, of whom it is written that the way was in their hearts."

"But God the Father is so little to me!"

"But to deal with Christ is to deal with God: to be wrapped up in the love of Christ is to make ever deeper discoveries into the heart of God. He is the Way to God: to know Him is to come to the Father."

**Christ as the Truth** The thought grows deeper as we advance. Obedience to the Way conducts to the vision of the Truth; ethics to spiritual optics. The truth seeker must first submit himself in all humility and obedience to Christ; and when he is willing to do His will, he is permitted to know.

*Christ is more than a teacher.* "We know that thou art a teacher come from God," said Nicodemus (John 3:2). He is more, He is the Truth of God. All truth is wrapped up in Him. All the mysteries of wisdom and knowledge are hidden in Him. We fully know truth only as it is in Jesus. When the Spirit of Truth would lead us into all truth, He can do nothing better than take of the things of Christ, and reveal them to us, because to know Christ is to know the truth in its most complete, most convenient, and most accessible form. If you know Christ intimately and fully, even if you know nothing else, you will know the truth, and the truth will make you free. If you love truth, and are a child of the truth, you will be inevitably attracted to Christ, and recognize the truth that speaks through His glorious nature. "He that is of the truth heareth my voice" (John 18:37).

*Distinguish between Christ the Truth and truth about Him.* Many true things may be said about Him; but we are not saved by truths about Him, but by Himself, the Truth.

Not the indubitable fact that Jesus died; but the Person of Him who died and lives for evermore.

Not the certain fact that Jesus lay in the grave; but the blessed Man Himself, who lay there for me.

Not the incontestable facts of His resurrection and ascension; but that He has borne my nature to the midst of the throne, and has achieved a victory that helps me in my daily struggle.

This is the ground basis of all true saving faith. The soul may accept truths about Christ, as it would any well authenticated historical facts; but it is not materially benefited or saved until it has come to rest on the bosom of Him of whom these facts are recorded.

*To know Christ as Truth demands truth in heart and life.* The insincere man; the trifler; the flippant jester, who takes nothing seriously; the superficial man, who uses the deepest expressions as counters for society talk; the inconsistent man, who is daily doing violence to his convictions by permitting things that his conscience condemns—must stand forever on the outskirts of the temple of truth: they have no right to stand before the King of truth. If you have never discerned the truth as it is in Jesus, it becomes a serious question whether you are perfectly true, or whether you are not, like Pilate, harboring insincerity in your heart, which blinds your eyes to His ineffable attributes.

*Concern yourself with Christ.* Be content to let the world and its wisdom alone. "The wisdom of this world is foolishness with God. . . He taketh the wise in their own craftiness" (1 Cor. 3:19). Give yourself to know Christ, who is made unto us wisdom, as well as sanctification and redemption. To know Him is to be at the fountain head of all truth; and the soul that has dwelled with Him day and night will find itself not only inspired by an undying love for the true, but able to hold fellowship with truth lovers and truth seekers everywhere; nay, will be able even to instruct those who have the reputation of great learning and knowledge in the schools of human thought. "I have more understanding than all my teachers: for thy testimonies are my meditation. I understand more than the ancients, because I keep thy precepts" (Ps. 119:99-100). To know and to possess Christ is to have the Word, that is the Wisdom of God, enshrined as a most sacred possession in the heart.

**Christ as the Life**

It is not enough to know; we need life. Life is, indeed, the gate to knowledge. "This is life eternal, that they should know thee." It was imperative, therefore, that Jesus should become a source of life to men, that they might know the Truth, and be able to walk in the Way; and more especially since death had infected and exhausted all the springs of the world's vitality.

It was into a world of death that the Son of God came. The spring of life in our first parents had become tainted at its source. At the best Adam was only a living soul. Dead—dead—dead in trespasses and sins; such was the divine verdict, such the course of this world. Earth resembled the valley in the prophet's vision, full of bones, very many and very dry. All the reservoirs of life were spent; its fountains had died away in wastes of sand.

Then the Son of God brought life from the eternal throne, from God Himself; and became a life-giving Spirit. His words were spirit and life: He was Himself the Resurrection and the Life: those who believed in Him became partakers of the divine nature. The tree of life was again planted in the earth's soil, when Jesus became incarnate. "I give eternal life unto my sheep," He said, "and they shall never perish." "He that believeth on the Son hath eternal life."

If, then, you are wanting life, and life more abundantly, you must have Christ. Do not seek *it*, but *Him:* not the stream, but the fountain; not the word, but the speaker; not the fruit, but the tree. He is the Life and Light of men.

And if you have Christ, you have life. You may not be competent to define or analyze it; you may not be able to specify the place or time when it first broke into your soul; you may hardly be able to distinguish it from the workings of your own life: but if you have Christ, trust Christ, desire Christ above all, you have the Life. "He that hath the Son hath life; he that hath not the Son of God hath not life. . . . We know him that is true, and we are in him that is true . . . this is eternal life" (1 John 5:12, 20). "I," said Jesus, "am the way, the truth, and the life."

# 6 *Christ Revealing the Father*

*Philip saith unto Him, Lord, shew us the Father, and it sufficeth us. Jesus saith unto him . . . He that hath seen Me hath seen the Father.*

*John 14:8, 9*

The Longing of the universal heart of man was voiced by Philip, when he broke in, rather abruptly, on our Lord's discourse with the challenge that He should answer all questions, dissipate all doubt, by showing them the Father. Is there a God? How can I be sure that He is? What does He feel toward us? These are questions that men persistently ask, and wait for the reply. And the Master gave the only satisfactory answer that has ever been uttered in the hearing of mankind, when He said in effect, "The knowledge of God must be conveyed, not in words or books, in symbols or types, but in a life. To know Me, to believe in Me, to come into contact with Me, is to know the deepest heart of God. He that hath seen Me hath seen the Father; how sayest thou then, 'Show us the Father'?"

**Philip's Inquiry** *It bore witness to the possible growth of the human soul.* Only three short years before, as we are told in the first chapter of this Gospel, Christ had found him. At that time he was probably much as the young men of his age and standing. Not specially remarkable save for an interest in, and an earnestness about, the advent of the Messiah; his views, however, of His person and work were limited and narrow: he looked for His advent as the time for the reestablishment of the kingdom of David, and deliverance from the Roman yoke. But three years of fellowship with Jesus had made a wonderful difference in this young disciple. The deepest mysteries of life and death and heaven seemed within his reach. He is not now content with beholding the Messiah; he is eager to know the Father, and to stand within the inner circle of His presence chamber.

The highest watermark ever touched by the great soul of Moses was when he said, amid the sublimities of Sinai, "I beseech thee, show my thy glory" (Exod. 33:18). But in this aspiration Philip stands beside him. There is a close kinship between the mighty lawgiver and the fisherman of Bethsaida. How little there is to choose between, "Show me thy glory," and "Show us the Father." Great and marvelous is the capacity of the soul for growth!

*It truly interpreted the need of man.* "It sufficeth us." From nature, with all her voices that speak of God's power and godhead; from the page of history, indented with the print of God's footprints; from type and ceremony and temple, though instituted by God Himself; even from the unrivaled beauty of our Savior's earthly life—these men turned unsatisfied, unfilled, and said, "We are not yet content; but if You would show us the Father, we would be."

And would it not suffice *us?* Would it not be sufficient to give new zest and reality to *prayer,* if we could realize that it might be as familiar as the talk of home, or like the petitioning of a little child? Would it not suffice to make the most irksome *work* pleasant, if we could look up and discern the Father's good pleasure and smile of approval? Would it not suffice to rob *pain* of its sting, if we could detect the Father's hands adjusting the heat of the furnace? Would it not suffice to shed a light across the dark mystery of *death,* if we felt that the Father was waiting to lead us through the shadows to Himself? How often the cry rises from sad and almost despairing hearts, "Show us the Father, and it sufficeth us."

*But surely this request was based on a mistake.* Philip wanted a visible theophany, like that which Moses beheld when the majestic procession swept down the mountain pass; or as the elders saw when they beheld the paved sapphire work; or after the fashion of the visions granted to Elijah,

Isaiah, or Ezekiel. He wanted to see the Father. But how can you make wisdom, or love, or purity visible, save in a human life?

Yet this is the mistake we are all liable to make. We feel that there must be an experience, a vision, a burst of light, a sensible manifestation, before we can know the Father. We strain after some unique and extraordinary presentation of the Deity, especially in the aspect of fatherhood, before we can be completely satisfied, and thus we miss the lesson of the present hour. Philip was so absorbed in his quest for the transcendent and sublime, that he missed the revelations of the Father which for three years had been passing under his eyes. God had been manifesting His tenderest and most characteristic attributes by the beauty of the Master's life, but Philip had failed to discern them; the Master now bids him go back on the photographs of those years, as fixed in his memory, to see in a thousand tiny illustrations how truly the Father dwelt in Him, and lived through His every word and work.

Are you straining after the vision of God, startled by every footstep, intently listening until the very atmosphere shall become audible, expecting an overwhelming spectacle? In all likelihood you will miss all. The kingdom does not come with outward show. When men expected Christ to come by the front door, He stole in at the back. While Philip was waiting for the Father to be shown in thunder and lightning, in startling splendor, in the stately majesty that might become the Highest, he missed the daily unfolding of the divine nature that was being afforded in the life with which He dwelt in daily contact.

*Philip's request emphasized the urgent need of the ministry of the Holy Spirit.* "If ye had known me . . ." the Savior said. "Have I been so long time with you, and yet hast thou not known me?" The disciples failed to know the Father, because they failed to know Christ; and they failed in this because they knew Him only after the flesh. They were so familiar with Him as their Friend, His love was so natural, tender, and human, He had become so closely identified with all their daily existence, that they did not recognize the fire that shone behind the porcelain, the deity that tabernacled beneath the frail curtains.

Often those who dwell amid the loveliest or grandest scenery miss the beauty that is unveiled to strangers from a distance. Certain lives have to be withdrawn from us before we understand how fair they were, and how much to us. And Jesus had to leave His disciples before they could properly appreciate Him. The Holy Spirit must needs take of the things of Christ, and reveal them, before His followers could realize their true significance, symmetry, and beauty.

Two things are needful, then: first, we must know Christ through the teaching of the Holy Spirit; and next, we must receive Him into our hearts, that we may know Him, as we know the workings of our own hearts. Each knows himself, and could recognize the mint mark of his own individuality; so when Christ has become resident within us, and has taken the place of our self-life, we know Him as we know ourselves. "What man knoweth the things of a man, save the spirit of man which is in him? . . . but we have the mind of Christ" (1 Cor. 2:11, 16).

**The Lord's Reply**

"He that hath seen me hath seen the Father."

He did not rebuke the request, as unfit to proffer, or impossible to satisfy. He took it for granted that such a desire would exist in the heart, and that His disciples would always want to be led by Him into the Father's presence. In this His ministry resembled that of the great forerunner, who led His disciples into the presence of the Bridegroom, content to decrease if only He might increase. The Master's answer was, however, widely different from John's. The forerunner pointed to Jesus as He walked, and said, "Behold the Lamb of God"; Jesus pointed to Himself, and said, "I and my Father are One; to have seen Me is to have seen the Father; to have Me is to possess the Father."

It troubled the Lord greatly that He had been with His disciples for such a long time, and yet they had not known Him; that they had not realized the source of His words and works; that they had concentrated their thought on Him, instead of passing, as He meant them to do, from the stream to the source, from the seal to the die, from the beam of the divine glory to its Sun. He urged them therefore from that moment to realize that they knew and had seen the Father in knowing and seeing Himself. Not more surely had the Shekinah dwelt in the tabernacle of old, than it indwelled His nature, though too thickly shrouded to be seen by ordinary and casual eyes.

Let us get help from this. Many complain that they know Christ, pray to Christ, are conscious of Christ, but that the Father is far away and impalpable. They are therefore straining after some new vision or experience of God, and undervaluing the religious life to which they have already attained. It is a profound mistake. To have Jesus is to have God; to know Jesus is to know God; to pray to Jesus is to pray to God. Jesus is God manifest in the flesh. Look up to Him even now from this printed page, and say, "My Lord and my God."

Jesus is not simply an incarnation of God in the sense in which, after the fashion of the Greek mythology, gods might come down in the likeness of men, adopting a disguise which they would afterward cast aside; Jesus *is* God. All the gentle attributes of His nature are God's; and all the strong and awful attributes of power, justice, purity, which we are wont to associate with God, are His also.

Happy is the moment when we awake to realize that in Jesus we have God manifest and present; to know this is the revelation of the Father by the Son, of which our Savior spoke in Matthew 11:27.

**A Glimpse Into the Lord's Inner Life**

This Gospel is the most lucid and profound treatise in existence on His inner life. It is the revelation of the principles on which our Savior lived.

So absolutely had He emptied Himself that He never spake His own words: "The words that I speak unto you I speak not of myself." He never did His own works: "My Father worketh hitherto, and I work. . . . The Father abiding in me doeth his works" (John 5:17; 14:10). This was the result of that marvelous self-emptying of which the apostle speaks. Our Lord speaks as though, in His human nature, He had a choice and will of His own. "Not my will, but thine be done," was His prayer. Perhaps it was to this holy and divine personality that Satan made appeal in the first temptation, bidding Him use His powers for the satisfaction of His hunger, and in independence of His Father's appointment. But however much of this independence was within our Lord's reach, He deliberately laid it aside. Before He spoke, His spirit opened itself to the Father, that He might speak by His lips; before He acted, He stilled the promptings of His own wisdom, and lifted Himself into the presence of the Father, to ascertain what He was doing, and to receive the inflow of His energy (John 5:19; 12:44, 49).

These are great mysteries, which will engage our further consideration. In the meanwhile, let us reason that if our Lord was so careful to subordinate Himself to the Father that He might be all in all, it well becomes us to restrain ourselves, to abstain from speaking our own words or doing our own works, that Jesus may pour His energies through our being, and that those searching words may be fulfilled in us also, "Striving according to his working, which worketh in me mightily" (Col. 1:29).

# 7 *The Great Deeds of Faith*

*Verily, verily, I say unto you, He that believeth on me, the works that I do shall he do also; and greater works than these shall he do; because I go unto my Father.*

*John 14:12*

Whenever our Lord was about to say something unusually important, He introduced it by the significant expression, "*Verily, verily*"; or, as it is in the original, "Amen, amen, I say unto you." The words well become His lips, who in the Book of Revelation is called "the Amen, the Faithful and True Witness." They are really our Lord's most solemn affirmation of the truth of what He was about to utter, as well as an indication that something of importance was about to be revealed.

Indeed, it was necessary in the present case that the marvelous announcement of the text should receive unusual confirmation, because of its wide extent. If our Lord had ascribed this power of doing greater works than He achieved in His earthly life, to apostle, prophet, or illustrious saint, we should have required no special assurance of its deliberate truth; but to learn that powers so transcendent are within the reach of any ordinary believer, to learn that anyone who believes may outdo the miracles on the outskirts of Nain and at the tomb of Bethany, is as startling as it is comforting. There is no reason why the humblest soul that ponders this page should not become the medium and vehicle through which the Christ of the glory shall not surpass the Christ of Galilee, Jerusalem, and Judea.

The best method of treating these words is to take them clause by clause as they stand.

**The First Note Is Faith**

"He that believeth on me." Three varieties of faith are alluded to in the context. Faith in His works: "Believe the works." Faith in His words: "Believe me." Faith in Himself, as here. In the Greek the preposition translated *in,* would be better rendered *into,* as though the believer was ever approaching the heart of Christ in deeper, warmer, closer fellowship; perpetual motion *toward,* combined with unbroken rest *in.* Each of these three forms of faith plays an important part in the Christian life.

Arrested by the works of Christ—His irresistible power over nature, His tender pity for those who sought His aid, the blessed and far-reaching results of His miracles—we cry with Nicodemus, "Verily, this is a Teacher come from God; for none can do such miracles, except God be with him" (John 3:2). The Master perpetually appealed to the witness borne by His works to His divine mission; as when He said, "If I had not done among them the works which none other man did, they had not had sin; but now have they both seen and hated both me and my Father" (John 15:24). And again, "The same works that I do bear witness of me" (John 5:36). But at the best the works of Christ are only like the great bell ringing in the church tower calling attention to the life being unfolded within, and are not calculated to induce the faith to which the greater works are possible.

Next we come to the words of Christ. They are spirit and life: they greatly feed the soul. He speaks as none other has ever spoken of the mysteries of life, death, God, and eternity. It is through the words that we come to the Speaker. By feeding on them we are led into vital union with Himself. But His words, as such, and apart from Him, will not produce works that shall surpass those He wrought in His earthly ministry.

Therefore from works and words we come to the Lord Himself with a trust that passes up beyond the lower ranges of faith; which does not simply receive what He waits to give, or reckon on his faithfulness, but which unites us in indissoluble union with Himself. This is the highest function of faith; it is *unitive:* it welds us in living union with our Lord, so that we are one with Him, as He is one with God.

We are in Him in the divine purpose that chose us in Him before the foundation of the world; grafted into Him in His cross; partaking of a common life with Him through the regeneration of the Holy Spirit. But all these become operative in the union wrought by a living faith, so that the strongest assertions that Jesus made of the close relationship between His Father and Himself become the current coin of holy speech, as they precisely describe the union that subsists between us and Jesus. The living Savior has sent us, and we live by the Savior. The words we speak are not from ourselves; but the Savior within us, He does His works. We are in Him, and He in us; all ours are His, and His ours.

Stay, reader and ask yourself whether you have this faith that incorporates you with the Man who died for you on the cross, and now occupies the throne—the last Adam who has become a lifegiving Spirit.

**A True Faith Always Works**

"He that believeth on me, the works that I do shall he do also."

There are many counterfeits of faith in the world. But they will inevitably fail in the supreme test, if not before. The apostle James especially calls attention to the distinction between a living and a dead faith. It becomes us to be on our guard.

The test of genuine faith is twofold. In the *first* place, a genuine, living faith has Christ for its object. The hand may tremble, but it touches His garment's hem; the eye may be dimmed by doubt, but it is directed toward His face; the feet may stumble, but as the fainting pilgrim staggers onward this is his repeated cry, "Thou, O Christ, art all I want."

In the *second* place, a true faith works. Its works approve its nature, and show that it has reached the heart of Christ, and has become the channel through which His life forces pour into the soul. Jacob knew that Joseph was alive and that his sons had opened communications with him, because of the wagons that he sent; and we may know that Jesus lives beyond the mist of time, and that our faith has genuinely connected us with Him, because we feel the pulse of His glorious nature within our own. And when this is so, we cannot but work out what He is working within.

Do you ask me why a true faith must work? Ask why the branch can do no other than bear clusters of ruddy grapes; its difficulty would be to abstain from bearing; the vitality of the root accounts for its life and productiveness. Blame the lark, whose nature vibrates in the sunshine, for pouring from its small throat volumes of sound; blame the child, full of bounding health, for laughing, singing, and leaping; blame the musician, whose soul has caught some fragments of the music of eternity, for pouring it forth in song—before you wonder why it is that the true faith that has opened the way from the believer to His Lord produces those greater works.

**There Are Two Kinds of Work Indicated**

*"The works that I do shall he do also."* What a blessing Christ's ministry must have been to thousands of sufferers! He passed through Galilee as a river of water of life. In front of Him were deserts of fever blasted by the sirocco, and malarious swamps of ague and palsy, and the mirage of the sufferer's deferred hope; but after He had passed, the parched ground became a pool and the thirsty land springs of water, the eyes of the blind were opened and the ears of the deaf unstopped, the lame man leaped as a deer and the tongue of the dumb sang.

How glad the sick of any district must have been when it was rumored that He was on His way to it! What eager consultations must have been held as to the best means of conveying them into His presence! What sleepless nights must have been spent in speculation as to whether, and how, He would heal!

Such results followed the labors of the apostles. The lame man at the beautiful gate of the Temple; the palsied Aneas; the dead Dorcas; the crowds in the streets overshadowed by Peter's passing figure; the miracles wrought by Paul at Paphos, Lystra, Philippi, and Malta—all attested the truth of the Master's words, "The works that I do shall he do also." There is no doubt that, if it were necessary, such miracles might be repeted, if only the church exercised the same faith as in those early days of her ministry to the world. But there are greater works than these.

*"Greater works than these shall he do."* The soul is greater than the body, as the jewel than the casket. All work, therefore, which produces as great an effect on the soul life as miracles, on the physical life must be proportionately greater as the tenant is greater than the house, as the immortal than the mortal. It is a greater work to give sight to the blind soul than to the blind body; to raise the soul from its grave than Lazarus from his four days' sleep.

Again, eternity is also greater than time, as the ocean is greater than a creek. The ills from which the miracles of Christ delivered the suppliant crowds were at the most limited by years. The flesh of the leper became wrinkled with old age; Jairus' daughter died again; the generation that had benefited from the mighty works passed away without handing on a legacy of health to succeeding time! But if a sinner is turned from the error of his ways, if salvation comes to a nature destined for immortality, and lifts it from the slough of sin to the light of God, the results must be greater because they are more permanent and far-reaching.

Moreover, the pain from which the word of the gospel may save is infinitely greater than that which disease could inflict. Men have been known to brave any physical torture rather than endure the insupportable anguish of a sin-laden conscience. The worm that never dies is more tolerable than cancer; the fire that is never quenched keener than that of fever. To save a soul from these is therefore a greater work.

Christ hinted at this distinction in one of His earliest miracles, when He proposed to forgive the sick of the palsy his sins, before bidding him walk; and bade the seventy rejoice more that their names were written in heaven than that the devils were subject to them. The apostles bear witness to a growing appreciation of this distinction, by the small space given in the Book of Acts to their miracles, compared with the greater attention concentrated on their discourses; and surely the history of Christendom bears witness to the great and permanent character of spiritual work. The church could not have influenced the world as she has done, had she been nothing more than a healer of diseases and an exorciser of demons.

**The Source of These Greater Works**

"Because I go unto my Father." Clearly the church has had an argument to present to men which even her Master could not use. He could not point, except indefinitely, to the cross, its flowing blood, its testimony to a love that the cold waters of death could not stanch. Through the ages this has been the master motive, the supreme argument.

Then, again, the Master could not count as we can on the cooperation of the Spirit in His convicting power. "When he is come, he will reprove the world of sin" (John 16:8); but He did not come until after that brief career of public ministry had closed. Speaking reverently, we may say that the church has an Ally that even her Master did not have.

But the main reason is yet to come. Perhaps an illustration will best explain it. Suppose the greater painter, Raphael, were to infuse his transcendent power, as he possessed it during his mortal life, into some young brain, there is no reason why the genius of the immortal painter should not effect, through a mere tyro in art, results in form and color as marvelous as those that he bequeathed to coming time. But suppose, further, that after having been amid the tones, forms, and colors of the heavenly world he could return and express his thoughts and conceptions through some human medium. Would not these later productions be greater works than those that men cherish as a priceless legacy? So if the Lord were to work in us such works only as He did before He ascended to His glory, they would be inferior to those that He can produce, now that He has entered into His glorified state, and has reassumed the power of which He emptied Himself when He stooped to become incarnate. This is what He meant when He said, "Because I go unto the Father."

Open your hearts to the living, risen, glorified Savior. Let Him live freely in your life, and work unhindered through your faith. Expect Him to pour through you as a channel some of those greater works that must characterize the closing years of the present age. Remember how the discourses and miracles of His earthly life ever increased in importance and meaning; for such must be the law of His ministry in the heavenlies. According to our faith it will be unto us. The results that we see around us are no measure of what Christ would or could do; they indicate the straitening effect of our unbelief. Lift up your heads, O ye gates, and be ye lifted up, ye low-browed doors of unbelief; and the King of Glory shall come in with His bright and mighty retinue, and shall go out through human lives to do greater works by the instrumentality of His people than ever He did in the course of His earthly ministry.

# 8 How to Secure More and Better Prayer

*And I will pray the Father, and he shall give you another Comforter, that he may abide with you for ever.*

*John 14:16*

The great lack of our life is that we do not pray more. And there is no failure so disastrous or criminal as this. It is very difficult to account for it. If in all times of discouragement and vicissitude we could have access to one of the wisest and noblest of our fellow creatures, or to some venerated departed saint, or to the guardian angel deputed to attend our steps, or to the archangel that presides as viceregent over this system of worlds, how strong and brave we should become! Whatever our need, we would at once seek his august presence, and obtain his counsel and assistance. How extraordinary is our behavior then with respect to prayer, and that we make so little of our opportunities of access into the presence of our Father, in whom wisdom, power, and love blend perfectly, and who is always willing to hear us—nay, is perpetually urging us to come!

The reason may lie in the very commonness of our opportunities. The door of prayer stands always waiting for the least touch of faith to press it back. If our Father's presence chamber were opened to us only once a year, with how much greater reverence would we enter it, how much more store would we set on it! We should anticipate for the whole year the honor and privilege of that interview, and eagerly avail ourselves of it. Alas, that familiarity with prayer does not always increase our appreciation of its magnificence!

The cause of our apathy is probably also to be sought in the effort that is required to bring our sensuous and earthbound natures into true union with the Spirit of God. True prayer is labor. Epaphras labored in his intercessions. Our feet shrink from the steep pathway that climbs those heights; our lungs do not readily accustom themselves to the rare air that breathes around the summit of the Mount of Communion.

But there is a deeper reason yet: we have not fully learned or obeyed the laws and conditions of prayer. Until they are apprehended and complied with, it is not possible for us to pray as we might. They are not, however, very difficult. The least advanced in the divine school may read them on this page, where Christ unbares the deepest philosophy of devotion in the simplest phrases.

It is evident that He expected that the age which Pentecost was to inaugurate, and to which He so frequently refers as "in that day," would in a special sense be the age of prayer. Mark how frequently in this last discourse He refers to it (14:13, 14; 15:7, 16; 16:24, 26). Clearly the infilling of the Holy Spirit has a special bearing on the prayerfulness of the individual and the church. But this will unfold as we proceed.

**The Praying Christ**

"I will pray the Father." It is true that He sat down at the right hand of the Majesty on high, because He had completed the work for which He became man. That session indicated a finished atonement. As the Father rested from the work of creation, so the Son entered into His rest, having ceased from the work of redemption, so far as it could be effected in His death, resurrection, and ascension. But as the Father in His rest worked in providence, sustaining that which He had created, so did the Savior continue to work after He had entered into His Sabbath keeping.

We have already dealt with one branch of his twofold activity, in *his work through those who believe.* The greater works that the risen Savior has been, and is, achieving through His people bear witness to the perpetual energy streaming from His life in the azure depths. "The apostles," Mark tells us, "went forth and preached every where, the Lord working with them, and confirming their word with signs following" (16:20).

The other branch of his twofold ministry is *his intercession on our behalf.* He says, "I will pray the Father" for you.

(1) What a contrast to the assertions that we have already pondered of His oneness with the Father, and to His assurance in almost the same breath that He would Himself answer His people's prayers! It is inexplicable, save on the hypothesis that He has a dual nature, by virtue of which, on the one hand, He is God, who answers prayer, and on the other the Son of Man, who pleads as the Head and Representative of a redeemed race.

(2) It is, however, in harmony with Old Testament symbolism. The high priest often entered the presence of God with the names of the people on his breast, the seat of love, and on his shoulder, the seat of power; and once a year, with a bowl of blood and sprig of thyme in his hands, pleaded for the entire nation. What more vivid portrayal could there be of the ceaseless intercession of that high priest who was once manifested to bear the sin of many, and who now appears in the presence of God for us!

(3) In the days of his flesh, He pleaded for His *church,* as in the sublime intercessory prayer of chapter 17; for *individuals,* as when He said, "Simon, Simon, Satan hath desired to have you, that he may sift you as wheat: but I have prayed for thee" (Luke 22:31); and for *the world,* as when He first assumed His high-priestly functions, saying from His cross, "Father, forgive them; for they know not what they do" (Luke 23:34). Thus He pleads still. For Zion's sake He does not hold His peace, and for Jerusalem's sake He does not rest. For His church, for individual believers, for you and me, He says in heaven, as on earth, "Father, I pray for them." Perennially from His lips pours out a stream of tender supplication and entreaty. This is the river that makes glad the city of God. Anticipating coming trial; interposing when the cobra coil is beginning to encircle us; pitying us when the sky is overcast and lowering; not tiring or ceasing, though we are heedless and unthankful—He pleads on the mountain brow through the dark hours, while we sleep.

(4) These intercessions are further stimulated by our love and obedience. "If ye love me, keep my commandments, *and*

I will pray the Father" (John 15:15, 16). He looks on us; and where love is yearning to love more fully, and obedience falters in its high endeavors, He prays yet more eagerly that grace may be given us to be what we long to be. He prays for those who do not pray for themselves; but He is even more intent on the perfecting of those who, because of their loyalty and love, are the objects of His special interest—"I pray for them; I pray not for the world" (John 17:9).

(5) His special petition is that we may receive the gift of Pentecost. "I will pray the Father, and he shall give you another Comforter." It would almost seem as though He spent the mysterious ten days between His ascension and Pentecost in special intercession that His church might be endued with power from on high. The pleading church on earth and the pleading Savior in heaven were at one. The two voices agreed in perfect symphony, and Pentecost was the Father's answer. The Savior prayed to the Father, and He gave another Comforter. Nor has He ceased in this sublime quest. It is not improbable that every revival of religion, every fresh and deeper baptism of the Spirit, every new infilling of individual souls, has been due to our Savior's strong cryings on our behalf. It may be that at this hour He is engaged in asking the Father that He would dower the universal church with another Pentecost; and if so, let us join Him in the prayer.

**The Praying Church**

"Whatsoever ye shall ask in my name."

(1) Prayer must be addressed to the Father. As soon as we utter that sacred name, the divine nature responds; and, to put it vividly, is on the alert to hear what we desire. A little child cannot utter a sigh however slight, a sob however smothered, without awakening the quick attention of its mother; and at the first whisper of our Father's name, He is at hand to hear and bless. Alas! we have too often grieved His Holy Spirit by a string of selfish petitions, or a number of formal platitudes. To the wonderment of angels, we thus fritter away the most precious and sacred opportunities. Be still, then, before you pray, to consider what to ask; order your prayers for presentation:

and be sure to begin the blessed interview with words of sincere and loving appreciation and devotion.

(2) The conditions of successful prayer are clearly defined in these words. There must be love to Christ and to all men; obedience to His will, so far as it is revealed; recognition of His mediation and intercession, as alone giving us the right to draw nigh; identification with Him, so as to be able to use His name; passionate desires for the Father's glory. Where these five conditions exist, there can be no doubt as to our receiving the petitions that we offer. Prayer that complies with these conditions cannot fail, since it is only the return tide of an impulse that has emanated from the heart of God.

(3) Note how the Savior lives for the promotion of His Father's glory. How often, during His earthly ministry, He declared that He was desiring and seeking this beyond all else! Though His prayer could only be granted by His falling into the ground to die, He never flinched from saying, "Father, glorify thy name." But here He tells us that through the ages as they pass He will still be set on the same quest. By all means He must glorify His Father; and if, in any prayer of ours, we can show that what we ask will augment the Father's glory, we are certain to obtain His concurrence and glad acquiescence. "That," He says, "will I do."

(4) We must pray "in his name." As the ambassador speaks in the name of queen and country; as the tax collector appeals in the name of the authorities; both deriving from their identification with their superiors an authority they could not otherwise exercise—so our words become weighted with a great importance when we can say to our Father, "We are so one with Jesus that He is asking in and through us; these words are His; these desires His; these objects those on which His heart is set. We have His sanction and authority to use His name." When we ask a favor in the name of another, that other is the petitioner, through us; so when we approach God in the name of Jesus, it is not enough to append His sacred name as a formula, but we must see to it that Jesus is pleading in us, asking through our lips, as He is asking through His own in the heart of the sapphire throne.

**The Link Between These Two**

"He shall give you another Comforter." The word "Comforter" might be rendered "Advocate." We have two Advocates: one with the Father, Jesus Christ the righteous, the other with us. As the one ascended, the other descended. As the one sat down at the right hand of God, the other rested on the heads and hearts of the company in the Upper Room. As the one has compassion on our infirmities, so the other helps our infirmities. As the one ever lives to intercede for us in heaven, so the other makes intercession in us for the saints with groanings that cannot be uttered.

This is the clue to the mystery of prayer. It is all-important that the church on earth should be in accord with its Head in its petitions before the throne. Of what avail is it for a client and advocate to enter an earthly court of justice unless they are in agreement? Of what use is it to have two instruments in an orchestra that are not perfectly in tune? And how can we expect that God will hear us unless we ask what is according to His will, and, therefore, what is in the heart and thought of Jesus?

This, then, is the problem that confronts us. How can we ascertain what Jesus is pleading for? We may guess it generally, but how be assured of it particularly? Who will tell us the direction in which the current of His mighty pleadings is setting, that we may take the same direction? These inquiries are answered in the ministry of the Holy Spirit. On the one hand, He fills and moves the Head, and on the other, His members. There is one Spirit of life between Jesus in the glory and His believing people everywhere. One ocean washes the shores of all natures in which the life of God is found.

Be still, therefore, and listen carefully to the voice of the Spirit of God speaking in your heart, as you turn from all other sounds toward His still small whisper, and He will tell you all. Coming, as He does, from the heart of Jesus, He will tell you His latest thought. In Him we have the mind of Christ. Then, sure that we are one with Him, and therefore with the Father, we shall ask what is according to His will to give. Prayer goes in an eternal circle. It begins in the heart of God, comes to us through the Savior and by the Spirit, and returns through us again to its source. It is the teaching of the raindrops, of the tides, of the procession of the year; but wrought out and exemplified in the practice of holy hearts.

# 9 The Other Paraclete

*He shall give you another Comforter.*

*John 14:16*

There was no doubt in our Lord's mind that His asking would be at once followed by the Father's giving. Indeed, the two actions seemed, in His judgment, indissolubly connected—"I will ask, and He shall give." From which we learn that prayer is a necessary link in the order of the divine government. Though we are assured that what we ask in God's purpose to communicate—that it lies in the heart of a promise, or in the line of the divine procedure—yet we must nevertheless make request. "Ye have not," said the apostle James, "because ye ask not" (James 4:2). "Ask," said the Master, His eye being open to the laws of the spiritual world, "and it shall be given you" (Matt. 7:7).

The prayer of the Head of the church was heard, and He received the Holy Spirit to bestow Him again. "Having received of the Father the promise of the Holy Spriit," said the apostle Peter, "he hath shed forth this, which ye now see and hear" (Acts 2:33). Thus the Holy Spirit is the gift of the Father, through the Son; though He is equal with each of the blessed Persons in the Trinity, and is with them to be worshiped and glorified.

**The Personality of the Holy Ghost**

That word, "another"—"He shall give you *another* Comforter"—is in itself sufficient to prove the divinity and personality of the Holy Spirit. If a man promises to send another as his substitute, we naturally expect to see a man like himself, occupying his place, and doing his work. And when Jesus foreannounced another Comforter, He must have intended a Person as distinct and helpful as He had been. A breath, an afflatus, an impersonal influence, could not have stood in the same category with Himself.

There are those who think that the Holy Spirit is to the Lord Jesus what a man's spirit is to his body; and imagine that our Lord simply intended that the spirit of His life teaching and self-sacrifice would brood over and inspire His followers; but this could not have fulfilled the promise of "the other Comforter." It would simply have been Himself over again—though no longer as a living Person; rather as the momentum and energy of a receding force that gets weaker and ever weaker as the ages pass. Thus the spirit of Napoleon or of Cæsar is becoming little more than a dim faint echo of footsteps that once shook the world.

Jesus knew how real and helpful He had been to His followers—the center around which they had rallied; their Teacher, Brother, Master, and He would not have tantalized them by promising another Paraclete, unless He had intended to announce the advent of One who would adjust Himself to their needs with that quickness of perception, and sufficiency of resource which characterize a personal leader and administrator. There were times approaching when the little band would need counsel, direction, sympathy, the interposition of a strong wise hand—qualities that could not be furnished by the remembrance of the past, fading like the colors on clouds when the sun has set; but which could only be secured by the presence of a strong, wise, ever-present personality. "I have been one Paraclete," said the Lord in effect; "but I am now going to plead your cause with the Father, that another Paraclete may take My place, to be My other self, and to abide with you forever."

There is no adequate translation for the word *paraclete.* It may be rendered comforter, helper, advocate, interpreter; but no one word suffices. The Greek simply means one whom you call to your side, in a battle, or a law court, to assist you by word or act. Such a One is Christ; such a One is the Holy Spirit. He is a definite Person whom you can call to, and lean on, and work with. If a man were drowning, he would not call to the wandering breath of the wind; but to any person who might be on the shore. The Spirit is One whom you can summon to your side; and it is therefore quite in keeping with Scripture to pray to the Holy Spirit. On the whole we are taught to direct prayer to the Father, through the Son, and as prompted by the Holy Spirit; but as a matter of practice and habit, it is indifferent which person in the Holy Trinity we address, for each is equally God. As the Father is God, so also is the Son, and so the Holy Spirit. In her hymns and liturgies the church has never hesitated to summon the Holy Spirit to her help.

It is in recognition of the personality of the Holy Spirit that the historian of the Acts of the Apostles quotes his solemn words, "Separate *me* Barnabas and Saul" (Acts 13:1); tells us that Ananias and Sapphira lied to Him (Acts 5); and records that the church at Jerusalem commenced its encyclical letter with the words, "It seeemed good to the Holy Spirit and to us" (Acts 15:28). Happy that body of Christians which has come to realize that the Holy Spirit is as certainly, literally, and personally present in its midst, as Jesus Christ was present when in the days of His flesh He tarried among men!

**A Sevenfold Parallel Between the Advents of the Two Paracletes**

*Each was in the world before His specific advent.* Long before His incarnation the delights of the Son of God were with men. In angel form, He visited their tents, spoke with them face to face, calmed their fears, and fought on their behalf. He trod the holy fields of Palestine with noiseless footfall that left no impress on the lightest sands, long before He learned to walk with baby feet, or bore His cross up Calvary.

So with the Holy Spirit. He brooded over chaos, strove with men before the Deluge, moved holy men to write the Scriptures, foreshadowed the advent of the Messiah, equipped prophets and kings for their special mission. In restraining evil, urging to good, preparing the way for Christ, the Holy Spirit found abundant scope for His energies. But His influence was rather external than internal; savored rather of gift than grace; and dealt more often with the few than with the many—with the great souls that reared themselves to heaven like Alpine summits touched with the fires of dawn, rather than with the generality of men, who dwelt in the valley of daily commonplace, enwrapped in the mists of ignorance and unbelief. It was to be the special prerogative of this age, that He should be poured out on *all* flesh, so that sons and daughters should prophesy, while servants and handmaidens participated in His gracious influences.

*The advent of each was previously announced.* From the Fall, the coming of the great Deliverer was foretold in type and sign, in speech and act; in history and prophecy. Indeed, as the time of the Incarnation drew nigh, as Milton tells us in his sublime ode on the Incarnation, surrounding nations had caught from the chosen people the spirit of expectancy, and the world was in feverish anticipation of the coming of its Redeemer. He was the Desire of all nations. All the ages, and all the family of man, accompanied Mary to Bethlehem, and worshiped with the Magi.

So with the Holy Spirit. Joel distinctly foretold that in the last days of that dispensation, God would pour out His Spirit—and His message is echoed by Isaiah, Zechariah, Ezekiel, and others—till Jesus came, who more specifically and circumstantially led the thoughts of His disciples forward to the new age then dawning, which should be introduced and signalized by the coming and ministry of the Spirit.

*Each was manifested in a body.* The Lord Jesus in that which was prepared for Him by the Father, and born of a pure virgin. We are told that He took on Him the form of a servant, and was made in the likeness of man. Similarly, the Holy Spirit became, so to speak, incorporate in that mystical body, the church, of which Jesus is the Head.

On the day of Pentecost, the 120 who were gathered in the Upper Room, and who, up to that time, had had no corporate existence, were suddenly constituted a church, the habitation and home of the divine Spirit. What the human body of Jesus was to the second person of the Holy Trinity, that the infant church was to the third; though it did not represent the whole body, since we must add to those gathered in the Upper Room many more in heaven and on earth, who by virtue of their union with the risen Christ constituted with them the Holy Catholic Church, which is His body, the fullness of Him who filleth all in all. "This," said the blessed Spirit "is my rest forever; here will I dwell, for I have desired it."

*Each was named before His advent* "They shall call his name Emmanuel" (Matt. 1:23). "His name shall be called Wonderful, Counsellor, The mighty God, The everlasting Father, The Prince of Peace" (Isa. 9:6). Thus was the Lord Jesus designated to loving hearts before His birth.

So also with the Holy Spirit. The last discourses of Jesus are full of appellatives, each setting forth some new phase of the Holy Spirit's ministry; some freshly-cut facet of His character. The Spirit of Truth; the Holy Spirit; the Paraclete; the Spirit of Conviction—such are some of the names by which He was to be known.

*Each was dependent on another.* Our Lord said distinctly, "The Son can do nothing of himself, but what he seeth the Father do" (John 5:19); and He said of the Holy Spirit, using the same preposition, "He shall not speak of himself; but whatsoever he shall hear, that shall he speak" (John 16:13).

What a conception is here! It is as though the Holy Spirit were ever listening to the divine colloquy and communion between the Father and the Son, and communicating to receptive hearts disclosures of the secrets of the Deity. The things that eye has not seen, nor ear heard, God has revealed to us by His Spirit; "for the Spirit searcheth all things, yea, the deep things of God" (1 Cor. 2:10).

*Each received witness.* The Father bore witness to His Son on three separate occasions. On the first, at His baptism, He said, "This is my beloved Son, in whom I am well pleased"; on the second, when the three apostles were with Him on the holy mount, and He received from the Father glory and honor; and on the third, when the inquiry of the Greeks reminded Him of his approaching death, and the voice from heaven assured Him that glory would accrue to the Father through His falling into the ground to die.

So in regard to the Holy Spirit. Seven times from the throne the ascended Lord summons those who have ears to hear what the Spirit says to the churches; as though to emphasize the urgent importance of His message, and the necessity of giving it our most earnest heed, lest we should drift past it.

*The presence of each is guaranteed during the present age.* "I am with you," said the Lord, and they were among the closing words of His posthumous ministry, "all the days, even unto the end of the age"; and here it is foretold that the Comforter would abide *during the age,* for so the phrase might more accurately be rendered.

This is especially the age of the Holy Spirit. He may be grieved, ignored, and rejected; but He will not cease His blessed ministry to the bride, until the Bridegroom comes to claim her for Himself. Oh, let us avail ourselves of His gracious presence to the utmost of our opportunity, that He may realize in us the full purpose of His ministry. Let us not pray for Him, as if in any degree He had been withdrawn, but as believing that He is as much with the church of today as on the day of Pentecost; as near us as when awestruck eyes beheld Him settling in flame on each meekly-bowed head.

The Lord said, "He shall remain with you to the end of the age." The age is not closed, therefore He must be with us here and now. There can be no waning of His grace or power. The pot of oil is in the church, only she has ceased to bring her empty vessels. The mine is beneath our feet, but we do not work it as of yesterday. The electric current is virbrating around, but we have lost the art of switching ourselves on to its flow. It is not necessary then for us to pray the Father that He should give the Holy Paraclete in the sense in which He bestowed Him on the day of Pentecost in answer to the request of our Lord. That prayer has been answered: the Paraclete is here; but we need to have the eyes of our heart opened to perceive, and the hand of our faith strengthened that we may receive Him.

The work of the Holy Spirit in and through us is conditioned by certain great laws, which call for our definite and accurate obedience. Not on emotion, nor on hysteric appeals, nor on excitement, but on obedience, does the power of God's Spirit pass into human hearts and lives. Therefore, let us walk in the paracletism of the Paraclete, continually in the current of His gracious influences, which will bear us on their bosom ever nearer to our Lord. Oh, to glorify Him; to know and love Him; to become passionately eager that all hearts should enthrone Him regardless of the personal cost it may involve!

# 10 The Three Dispensations

*The Spirit of truth; whom the world cannot receive, because it seeth him not, neither knoweth him: but ye know him; for he dwelleth with you, and shall be in you.*

*John 14:17*

They are lofty themes that we have been discussing in the foregoing pages; and just because they touch the highest matters of the spiritual life, they involve us in profound responsibility. It was because Capernaum had been exalted to heaven in privilege, that she should be cast down to hell. Of those to whom much is given, much is required. Better not to have know these truths of the inner life, if we are content to know them only by an intellectual apprehension, and make no effort to incorporate them into the texture of our character. Few things harden more certainly than to delight in the presentation of the mysteries of the kingdom, without becoming a child of the kingdom.

The object therefore that now engages us is less one of elucidation than of self-examination. Let us discern ourselves. Let us see whether we be in the faith. Let us expose soul and spirit to the discrimination of the Word of God, which is a discerner of the thoughts and intents of the heart.

**There Are Two Avenues of Knowledge: Perception and Reception**

"Whom the world cannot receive, because it seeth him not, neither knoweth him." Three things are specified as beyond the range of the world's power: it does not receive, it does not know, it does not see the things of the unseen and eternal world. It cannot see them, therefore it does not know them, and therefore does not receive them; and this is especially true of its attitude toward the Holy Spirit.

When the world hears of the Holy Spirit, it brings to bear upon Him those organs of cognition which it has been accustomed to apply to the objects of the natural world, and even to the human life of Christ. But, as might have been expected, these are altogether useless. It is as absurd to endeavor to detect the presence of the spiritual and eternal by the faculties with which we discern what is seen and temporal, as it would be to attempt to receive the impression of a noble painting by the sense of taste, or to deal with the problems of astronomy by the tests that are employed in chemical analysis. The world, however, does not realize its mistake. It persists in applying tests to the Spirit of God that may be well enough in other regions of discovery, but which are worse than useless here. "The natural man receiveth not the things of the Spirit of God . . . neither can he know them, because they are spiritually discerned" (1 Cor. 2:14). "Whom the world cannot receive, for it seeth him not, neither knoweth him" (John 14:17).

There was a touch of this worldly spirit even in Thomas, when he said, "Except I shall see in his hands the print of the nails . . . and thrust my hand into his side, I will not believe" (John 20:25); and insofar as the world-spirit is permitted to hold sway within us, our powers of spiritual perception will be blunted, and become infected with the tendency to make our intellect or imagination our sole means of apprehending divine truth.

There is a better way than this; and our Lord indicates it when He says, "Ye know him, for he abideth with you, and shall be in you." Pascal said, "The world knows in order to love: the Christian loves in order to know." The same thought underlies these words of Christ. The world attempts to see the Spirit, that it may know and receive Him; the child of God receives Him by an act of faith, that he may know Him.

An illustration of this habit is given in the story of Naaman. The spirit of the world whispered to him of the desirability of *knowing* that the waters of Israel possessed curative properties, before he committed himself absolutely to the prophet's directions; and if he had waited to know before bathing, he would have remained a helpless leper to the end of his days.

His servants, however, had a clearer perception of the way of faith, and persuaded him to dip seven times in the Jordan. He acted on the suggestion, dipped seven times, and his flesh became as that of a little child. Similarly we are called to act upon grounds that the world would hold to be inadequate. We hear the testimony of another; we recognize a suitability in the promises of the Scripture to meet the deep yearnings of our soul; we feel that the words and works of Jesus Christ constitute a unique claim for Him, and we open our hearts toward Him. In absolute humility and perfect obedience we yield to Him our whole nature. Though the night be yet dark, we fling wide our windows to the warm southwest wind coming over the sea. The result is that we begin to know, with an intuitive knowledge that cannot be shaken by the pronouncements of the higher criticism. We have received the Spirit, and our life after that is too short to unfold all that is involved in that unspeakable gift. We know Him because He abides with us, and is in us. No man knows the things of a man, save the spirit of man that is in him; and we can only know the Spirit of God when He has taken up His residence within us, and witnesses with our spirit, as One who is interwoven with the very texture of the inner life.

Consecration is therefore the key to this higher knowledge; and if any who read this page are yearning after a discernment of the things of God on which they may build the house of their faith amid the swirl of the storm and the beat of the wave of modern doubt, let them open their entire nature, humbly to receive and diligently to obey that Spirit whom Christ waits to give to all who seek.

**The Characteristic of this Dispensation**

"He shall be *in* you." It has been repeatedly said that creation is the work of the Father; redemption, of the Son; and regeneration, of the Holy Spirit. It may also be said that there are three dispensations: that of the Father, in the earlier history of mankind; that of the Son, culminating in our Lord's ascension; and that of the Holy Spirit, in which we are now living. In the history of the world these were successive; in the history of souls they may be contemporaneous. In the same house one member may be in the dispensation of the Father, another in that of the Son, and a third in that of the Holy Spirit. It is highly necessary, says the saintly Fletcher, that every good steward of the mysteries of God should be well acquainted with this fact, otherwise he will not rightly divide the word of life. There is peril lest we should give the truth of one order of dispensation to those who are living on another level of experience.

There is a remarkable illustration of this in the life of John the Baptist, who clearly realized the distinction on which we are dwelling, and used it with remarkable nicety when approached by various classes of character. When gentile soldiers came to him, in Roman regimentals, he merely bade them do violence to no man, and be content with their wages. When Jews came, he said, "Behold the Lamb of God!" To his eagle eye a further dispensation was unveiled to which he alluded when he said, "He shall baptize you with the Holy Spirit, and with fire." Similarly they to whom inquirers address themselves should diagnose their spiritual standing, that they may lovingly and wisely administer the truth suitable to their condition.

*The dispensation of the Father* includes those who hope that He has accepted and forgiven them, but have no clear perception of the atoning work of Christ; who are governed rather by fear than love; who tremble beneath the thunders of Sinai more often than they rejoice at the spectacle of Calvary; who are tossed to and fro between hope and despair; who desire the favor of God, but hesitate to speak confidently of having attained it. Such are to be found in churches where the gospel is veiled beneath heavy curtains of misconception and formalism. In the same class we might put men, like Cornelius, who in every nation fear God and work righteousness.

*The dispensation of the Son* includes those who clearly perceive His divine nature, and rejoice in His finished propitiation; they know that they are accepted in the Beloved; they receive His teachings about the Father; they submit to the rule of life which He has laid down; but they know comparatively little of the inner life, or of their oneness with Christ in resurrection and ascension; they understand little of what the apostle meant by speaking of Christ being formed in the soul; and, like the disciples at Ephesus, they know but little of the mission and infilling of the Holy Spirit.

*The dispensation of the Holy Spirit* includes those who have claimed their share in Pentecost. In their hearts the Paraclete dwells in sanctifying grace, on their heads He rests in mighty anointing. Those of the dispensation of the Son resemble Ruth the gleaner; those of the dispensation of the Spirit, Ruth the bride. Those dwell in Romans 7 and Hebrews 3; these in Romans 8 and Hebrews 4. For those the water has to be drawn from the well; in these it springs up to everlasting life. Oh to know the "in-ness" of the Holy Spirit. Know you not that Jesus Christ is in you by the Spirit—unless you be reprobate!

**The Tokens of the Indwelling**

We must distinguish here, as Dr. Steele suggests, between what are variable, and what are constant.

*These vary:* (1) The joy of realization, which is sometimes overpowering in its intensity, at other times like the ebbing tide.

(2) Agony for souls, which would be insupportable if it were permanent. Christ only asks us to watch in Gethsemane for one hour.

(3) Access in prayer. Sometimes the vision is face to face; at others, though we grasp as in Jacob's night wrestle, we cannot behold. Like Esther, we seem to wait in the antechamber. As the lark of which Jeremy Taylor speaks, we rise against the east wind.

(4) The openings of Scripture. The Bible does not seem to be always equally interesting. At times it is like the scented letter paper, smelling of aloes and cassia, bearing the handwriting we love; at others it resembles the reading book of the blind man, the characters in which, by constant use, have become almost obliterated, so as hardly to awake answering thought.

(5) The pressure of temptation. We sometimes think that we are getting out of the zone of temptation. The pressure is

so reduced that we think we shall never suffer again as we have done. Then, suddenly, it bursts upon us—as the fury of the storm, when, after an hour's cessation, it takes the mariner unawares.

All these symptoms are too variable to be relied upon for a diagnosis of our spiritual condition, or an evidence of the dispensation to which we belong.

*These are constant:* (1) The consciousness of being God's. This is to be distinguished from the outgoing of our faith and love toward God. At the beginning of our experience we hold Him; but as the Holy Spirit dwells more fully we realize that we are held by Him. It is not our love to God, but His love to us; not our faith, but His faithfulness; not the sheep keeping near the Shepherd, but the Shepherd keeping the sheep near to Himself. A happy sense steals over the heart, as over the spouse—"I am my beloved's, and his desire is toward me" (Song of Sol. 7:10).

(2) The supremacy of Jesus in the heart. There is no longer a double empire of self and Christ—as in the poor Indian who said to the missionary, "I am two Indians, good and bad"; but there is the undivided reign of Christ, who has put down all rule and authority and power—as in the case of Martin Luther, who said, "If any one should ask of my heart, Who dwells here? I should reply, Not Martin Luther, but Christ."

(3) Peace, which looks out upon the future without alarm, because so sure that Christ will do His very best in every day that lies hidden beneath the haze of the future; which forbears to press its will too vehemently, or proffer its request too eagerly, because absolutely certain that Jesus will secure the highest happiness possible, consistently with his glory and our usefulness to men.

(4) Love. When the Spirit of God really dwells within, there is a baptism of love that evinces itself not only in the household and to those naturally lovable, but goes out to all the world, and embraces in its tenderness such as have no natural traits of beauty. Thus the soft waters of the Southern Ocean lap against unsightly rocks and stretches of bare shingle.

Where love reigns in the inner chamber of the soul, doors

do not slam; bells are not jerked violently; soft tones modulate the speech; gentle steps tread the highways of the world, bent on the beautiful work of the messengers of peace; and the very atmosphere of the life is warm and sunny as an aureole. There is no doubt of the indwelling Spirit where there is this outgoing love.

(5) Deliverance from the love and power of sin, so that it becomes growingly distasteful, and the soul turns with loathing from the carrion on which it once fed contentedly. This begets a sense of purity, robed in which the soul claims kinship to the white-robed saints of the presence chamber, and reaches out toward the blessedness of the pure in heart who see God. There is still a positive rain of smut and filth in the world around; there is a recognition of the evil tendencies of the self-life, which will assert themselves unless graciously restrained; but triumphing above all is the purity of the indwelling Lord, who Himself becomes in us the quality for which holy souls eagerly long.

# 11 Three Paradoxes

*I will not leave you comfortless: I will come to you.*
*The world seeth me no more; but ye see me.*
*Because I live, ye shall live also.*

*John 14: 18, 19*

The Bible and the Christian life are full of paradoxes. Paul loved to enumerate them; they abound also in the discourses of our Lord. Here are three.

The Master had declared His purpose of leaving His apostles and friends and returning to His Father: but in the same breath He says, "I will not leave you desolate; I come to you."

Again, He had forewarned them that He would be hidden from them; yet now He tells them that they would still behold Him.

Further, with growing emphasis and clearness, He had unfolded His approaching death by the cruel Roman method of the cross; yet He claims the timeless life of an everpresent tense, and insists that their life will depend on His.

Absent, yet present; hidden, yet visible; dying, yet living and life-giving—such are the paradoxes of this paragraph in His marvelous farewell discourse; and they reveal three facts of which we may live in perpetual cognizance.

**We May Enjoy the Perpetual Recognition of the Advent of Christ**

"I will not leave you orphans [or desolate]: I come unto you" (RV). Note the majesty of those last words; they are worthy of Diety; He speaks as though He were always drawing near those He loves: "I come unto you."

*Christ is always present, yet He comes.*

The Creator had always been immanent in His universe, but He came in each creative act; the Lawgiver had been everpresent in the church in the wilderness, but He came down on Sinai, and His glory lit up the peaks of sandstone rock; the Deliverer was never for a moment absent from the side of the shepherd-king, but in answer to his cry for help He came down riding upon a cherub, flying on the wings of wind; the Holy Spirit had been in the world from the earliest days of prayer and inspired speech, but He came down from the throne to sit on each bowed head in lambent flame. So Christ is with us all the days, yet He comes. He will come at last to receive His own to Himself, and to judge the world; but He comes in dark and lonely hours that we may not be desolate.

For warm, sweet, tender, even yet
  A present help is He;
And faith has yet its Olivet,
  And love its Galilee.
The healing of his seamless dress
  Is by our beds of pain;
We touch Him in life's throng and press,
  And we are whole again.

*He comes when we need Him most.* When the storm is high, and the water is pouring into the boat; when the house is empty because the life that made it home has fled; when Jericho has to be attacked on the morrow, and the Jordan crossed; when lover and friend stand aloof; when light is fading before dimming eyes, and names and faces elude the grasp of the aged mind; when the last coal is turning to gray ash; when the rush of the river is heard in the valley below—Jesus says, I come. It is in the hour of desolation, when Lazarus has been in the grave four days already, that the glad tidings are whispered in the ear of the mourner, "The Master is come." "I will not leave you orphans," He said: "I come unto you." Oh, blessed orphanhood, it were well to be bereaved, to have such comforting!

*He pays surprise visits.* He does not always wait to be invited; but sometimes, when we lie sleeping with wakeful hearts, we hear His gentle voice calling to us, "Arise, my love, and come away." Then as we open the door, we are refreshed with the sweet-smelling myrrh that betrays His presence. How often when we have been losing ground, getting lukewarm and worldly, we have suddenly been made aware of His reviving presence, and He has said, I come. He comes, as the wood anemones and snowdrops (the most fragile and tender flowerets of spring) penetrate the hard ground to announce that the winter is over and gone, and that the time of the singing of birds is come.

*It is well to put ourselves in His way.* There are certain beaten tracks well-worn by his feet, and if we would meet Him we must frequent their neighborhood. Olivet, where He used to pray; Calvary, where He died; Joseph's garden, where He rose, are dear to Him yet. When we pray or meditate; when we commemorate His dying love at the memorial feast; when we realize our union with Him in death and resurrection; when we open our hearts to the breathing of the Holy Spirit—we put ourselves in His way, and are more likely to encounter Him when He comes. "To them that look for Him shall He appear," (Heb. 9:28). "Behold, the bridegroom cometh: go ye out to meet him" (Matt. 25:6)—but take the path by which He is sure to travel. Be in the Upper Room, with the rest of the disciples, so that you may not, like Thomas, miss Him when He comes.

*His footsteps are noiseless.* It is said of old, "Thy footsteps are not known" (Ps. 77:19); therefore we need not be surprised if He steal in upon us as a thief in the night, or as spring over the plain. There is no blare of trumpet or voice of herald; we cannot say, Lo here or Lo there; when the King comes there is no outward show. "He shall not strive, nor cry; neither shall any man hear his voice in the street" (Matt. 12:19).

"He entered not by the eyes," says St. Bernard, "for his presence was not marked by colour; nor by the ears, for there was no sound; nor by the touch, for He was impalpable. How then did I know that He was present? Because He was a quickening power. As soon as He entered, He awoke my slumbering soul. He moved and pierced my heart, which before was stony, hard, and sick. He began also to pluck up and destroy, to build and plant, to freshen the inner drought, to enlighten the darkness, to open the prison-house, to make the crooked straight and the rough smooth; so that my heart could bless the Lord with all that was within me."

Oh, lonely, desolate soul, open your door to Him; wait not on the alert to detect His entrance, only believe that He is there: and presently, and before you are ever aware, you will find a new fragrance distilling through the heart chamber, a new power throbbing in your pulse.

**We May Enjoy the Perpetual Recognition of the Presence of Christ**

"The world sees me no more; but ye see me." Nothing makes men so humble and yet so strong as the vision of Christ.

*It induces humility.* When Isaiah beheld His glory more resplendent than the sheen of the sapphire throne, he cried that he was undone; when Peter caught the first flash of His miraculous power gleaming across the waves of Galilee, just when the fish were struggling in the full net, he begged Him to depart, because he felt himself a sinful man; and when John saw Him on the Isle of Patmos, he fell at His feet as dead—though, surely, if any of the apostles could have faced Him unabashed, it would have been John.

This is especially noticeable in the Book of Job. Few books are so misunderstood. It is supposed to contain the description of the victory of Job's patience; in reality it delineates its testing and failure. It shows how he who was perfect, according to the measure of his light, broke down in the fiery ordeal to which he was exposed, and finally was forced to cry, "I have heard of thee by the hearing of the ear: but now mine eye seeth thee. Wherefore I abhor myself, and repent in dust and ashes" (Job 42:5-6).

Would you be humble? Would you know yourself a worm and no man? Would you see that you are undone, defiled, and helpless? Then ask the blessed Spirit to reveal Jesus in all His matchless beauty and holiness, eliciting the confession that you are the least of saints and the chief of sinners. This is no forced estimate, when we take into account the opportunities we have missed, the gifts we have misused, the time we have wasted, the light we have resisted, the love we have requited with neglect.

*It produces strength.* See that man of God prone on the floor of his chamber, shedding bitter tears of godly sorrow, not forgiving himself, although he knows himself forgiven; bowing his head as a bulrush, crying that he is helpless, broken, and at the end of himself—will he be able to stand as a rock against the beat of temptation, and the assault of the foe? Yes; for the same presence that is to him a source of humility in private, will inspire to great deeds of faith and heroism when he is called to stand in the breach or lead the assault.

It is this vision of the present Lord that, in every age of the church, has made sufferers strong. "The Lord is on my right hand, I shall not be moved," said one. "The Lord stood by me, and strengthened me," said another. In many a dark day of suffering and persecution; in the catacombs; in the dens and caves where Waldenses hid; on the hillsides where the Covenanters met to pray; in the beleaguered cities of the Netherlands; in prison and at the stake—God's saints have looked to Him, and been lightened, and their faces have not been ashamed. "Behold," said the first martyr, "I see the heavens opened, and the Son of man standing on the right hand of God" (Acts 7:56).

Oh, for more of the open vision of Jesus, ministered to us by the gracious Spirit! Would that His words, "Ye behold Me," were more often verified in our experience! He is always with us; and if only our eyes were not closed, we should behold Him with the quick perception of the heart. Indeed, the race can only be rightly run by those who have learned the blessed secret of looking off to Him. "We see Jesus."

It is a most salutary habit to say often, when one is alone, "Thou art near, O Lord"; "Behold, the Lord is in this place." We may not at first realize the truth of what we are saying. His presence may be veiled, as the forms of mountains swathed in morning cloud. But as we persist in our quest, putting away from us all that would grieve Him, and cultivating the attitude of pure devotion, we shall become aware of a divine presence that shall be more to us than a voice speaking from out of the Infinite.

**We May Enjoy the Perpeptual Recognition of the Living Christ**

"Because I live, ye shall live also." There are many life verses in this Gospel that shine like stars in the firmament of Scripture. For example—in the first chapter, that in the Word, as manifested to men, was *life*; and in the fifth chapter, that "as the Father had life in himself; he gave to the Son to have life also in himself." The Father is the fountain of life. Eternal life is ever rising up in His infinite Being with perennial vigor; and all things living, from the tiny humming birds in the tropical forest to the strongest archangel beside the sapphire throne, derive their being from Him. Thus we have seen ferns around a fountain, nourishing their fronds on its spray. All things owe their existence and continued being to the unmeasured life which has been from all eternity treasured up in God, and is ever flowing out from God.

This life was Christ's, in the mystery of the eternal Trinity, before the worlds were made; but it was necessary that He should receive it into His human nature, so as to become the reservoir and storehouse from which all who were one with Him might receive grace on grace. "I am come," He said, "that they might have life, and that they might have it more abundantly" (John 10:10) This life dwelled in Him during His earthly ministry, though comparatively few availed themselves of it; His death put it in circulation for all the world; the smitten rock yielded streams of living water; the last Adam became a life-giving Spirit; from His throne He proclaimed Himself as He who lives, though He became dead, and is alive for evermore.

*We live by His life.* Our life is as dependent on Him as a babe's on its mother. Would anything happen to Him, we would instantly feel the effect. We have no independent, self-derived, or self-sustained life. Apart from Him we wither.

*We live in His life.* The tiny streamlet of our being has joined His, is merged in it, and flows on together with it, to the great ocean of eternity. To us to live is Christ, both here and hereafter. Our aims and purposes are merged in His; we are enriched in all that enriches Him; gladdened by all that promotes His happiness and glory; made more than conquerors through our oneness with Him, in the victory that has overcome the world.

*We live because He lives in us.* At the moment of regeneration He came to indwell. He who has the Son has life; he who has life has the Son. It has pleased God to reveal His Son in us. We have found Him of whom Moses in the law and the prophets did write, and we have found Him in our hearts. Where do you dwell? we asked Him; and He replied, Come and see: and He manifested Himself as having become to us the inward principle of an endless life. Christ dwells deep in our heart, and we are beginning to comprehend the immensity of the divine love of which He is the exponent.

Let us draw on this life more confidently, availing ourselves of it perpetually in all our time of need—in all time of our sickness and of our wealth, in adversity and prosperity, in the hour of mortal anguish and the day of judgment; and finding what we could not do or bear or encounter, Jesus can do and bear and meet in and through us, to the Father's eternal glory.

Lord Jesus Christ, grow Thou in me,
And all things else recede.

# 12 *Many Mansions for God*

*If a man love me, he will keep my words: and my Father will love him, and we will come unto him, and make our abode with him.*

*John 14:23*

The Immanence of God! That God should be willing to make His home *with* man is much; but that He should be willing to come in—to indwell, occupy, and possess our nature—this is incomprehensible to the intellect, though it may be received and rejoiced in by the heart. This no subject for light and thoughtless speech. We touch on the profoundest mysteries of the Being of the Infinite, and the capacity of human nature. Be reverent, O my soul, in the consideration of such a theme; and take the shoes from off your feet, for the bush burns with fire!

It was owing to the question of Jude that the universal application of our Master's words is so clear. A day or two before, our Lord had entered Jerusalem amid the enthusiasm of the crowds, and the disciples fondly thought the long-expected time had arrived when He would manifest Himself to the world as the Messiah. "This is the beginning of the messianic reign," said each apostle in his secret heart, as the great procession passed over the shoulder of Olivet; and each began to wonder what special post would be allotted to him in the new empire that seemed so close at hand. These nascent hopes, however, had been rudely dissipated by our Lord's declaration that the world was to see Him no more qualified nevertheless by the promise, "But ye see me."

The apostles therefore were inclined to think that in some

special form the manifestations of His grace and glory would be confined to them. Hence Jude's question, "What is come to pass, Master, that you will manifest yourself to us, and not unto the world?" Jesus answered in effect, "Do not think that you and your friends are to have the exclusive rights of beholding and communing with Me. What I offer to you is open to all who believe, love, and obey. The gate that I throw open shall stand wide for all who choose to enter. The veil shall be rent, that any who fulfill the spiritual conditions may see the light, and hear the voice, and stand in the inner court. If a *man* love Me. . . ." Note those emphatic words, "a man"—any man; you and me.

**The Divine Immanence**

"We will make our abode." The word "abode" is here a translation of the Greek word that is rendered "mansions" in a former part of this chapter. "We will make our *mansion* with Him." God is willing to become the mansion of the soul that believes in Christ; but asks in return that such a person should prepare a guest chamber, and become a mansion in which He may dwell. As He steals with noiseless tread into the loving, believing heart, I hear Him say, "This is My rest forever; here will I dwell, for I have desired it."

*It is the Immanence of the Father.* Who is this of whom the Savior speaks? The infinite God! Time with all its ages is but the flash of a moment in His eternity! Space, "beyond the soar of angel wings," is but a corner in His dwelling place! Matter, with its ponderous mass, is but the light dust that will not affect the level of the scale! The mighty sun, which is the center of all worlds, is but a mote floating in the beam of His being! All the gathered wisdom of man, stored in the libraries of the world, is but as a glowworm's spark compared with the meridian light of his wisdom! O souls of men, consider how marvelous that such a One, whom the heavens cannot contain, who overflows their limits, will yet become the resident of our nature!

*Its motive is Love.* "The Father will love him." This is wonderful—the more so as we are told that His love toward us is identical with that which He has toward our Lord. Speaking of those who shall believe through His apostles' word, Jesus said, "That the world may know that you loved them even as you loved Me." That God should condescend to think about our planet, which is as a leaf in the forest of being; that He should deign to regard mankind, who, in comparison with the material universe, are as a colony of ants compared with the Himalaya, at the foot of which they may have built their home; that He should pity our race—this would be much. But that He should *love* the world, that He should *love* individuals belonging to our race, the He should love them with the love He has toward the Only-begotten—we could not have believed this unless we had been assured by the lips of infallible truth. But the supreme revelation that towers above the rest, like some great banyan tree amid the slender growth of the Indian forest, is that the Creator should indwell and find a mansion in the heart of His creatures.

*It is dual, yet one.* "We will come." We! Then, are there more than one? Who is this who dares class Himself with the supreme God within the limits of a common pronoun; that challenges the love and trust and obedience of man; that poses as King? The meekest and humblest of men. The One who, above all others of the human family, seems to have least to disturb or darken the incidence of the rays of truth upon His soul; who has cast a light on all the dark problems of human life, and could not possibly have been deceived in respect to His own nature. His conceptions of the holiness, greatness, and purity of God have stood out in unrivalled magnificence from all others whatsoever; yet it is He who in one small word couples His humanity with deity, His meekness with the infinite majesty, His personality with God's. Is not this proof enough that He was conscious of His divine nature? Is not the fact of His not counting it robbery to be equal with God evidence that He was God? What can they make of this *We,* who hold that He was only a good man and a great teacher? Good men are humble men; great teachers know best their own limitations.

It is in, and with, and through the Son, and by the Spirit, that the Father comes to indwell.

*It is the Immanence of the Son. To be loved by Him were*

*much!* "I will love him." His love is of the rarest quality. True and tender, strong and sweet, inexorable in its demands upon Himself, inexhaustible in its outflow toward the objects of His affectionate regard. Such love as He gave to John, who grew like Him beneath the magic power of that environment; as He gave to Mary, who perhaps most deeply understood Him; as He gave to Peter, winning him back from his waywardness—brings with it a heaven of bliss, for which a man may well be prepared to count all things but loss. But there is a bliss beyond all this. The Lover of men would indwell them!

*It is much that He should seek our love.* "He that loveth me." We might have supposed that He would have been satisfied with the vastness of His dominion, and the myriad bright spirits that wait on His word! But no; the thirst for love cannot be satisfied with gold, or bright angelic servants. As Isaac could not find a companion among those who tended the flocks that browsed over the fields of Canaan, or among the troops of slaves that gathered around his father's tents, but Eliezer must bring a bride from across the desert; so the Son of God must needs come as a suitor to our world to find His bride, who can share His inner thoughts and purposes. Here is a marvel indeed. As the village that provides the emperor's bride becomes famous, so earth, though it be least among her sister spheres, shall have the proud preeminence of having furnished from her population the spouse of the Lamb. But, great as this marvel is, it is followed by the greater, that the Immortal Lover is willing to tenant the poor hearts whose love at the best is so faint and cold.

*It is much that He should give us manifestation of His love.* "I will manifest myself unto him." Have you not sometimes taken up a daisy, and looked into its little upturned eye, and thought and thought again, until through the gate of the flower you have passed into an infinite world of life, beauty, and mystery? There are moments when even a flower is transfigured before us, and manifests itself to us as a thought of God, a ray of His glory, the frail product of His infinite mind, the wick around which trembles the fire of the Shekinah! Have you not sometimes stood alone amid mountains, glaciers, wooded valleys, and rushing streamlets, until nature has dropped her veil, and revealed herself in a phase of beauty and a depth of meaning which struck you as altogether unique and singular? So there are moments in the life of the believer, when Christ, who is ever with us, manifests Himself as He does not to the world. There is borne in upon the spirit a consciousness that He is near; there is a waft of His breath, a savor of His fragrant dress, fresh from the ivory palaces.

All this is much: but how much more to be told that this glorious Christ, the Fellow of Jehovah, who with the Father and the Spirit is God; the Organ of creation; the Mouthpiece of the Godhead; the Mediator of Redemption; the Monarch of all worlds; the Supreme Teacher, Guide, and Savior of men—is prepared to repeat the experiences of Bethlehem, and make His abode in man! "*We* will come unto him, and make our abode with him."

*Learn to revere the work of God in the souls of others.* "For thy meat," said the apostle, "destroy not the soul for whom Christ died." He might have added, "and in whom Christ lives." Weak and erring, trying and vexatious, that fellow believer may be, yet there is a chamber in his nature in which God has already taken up His abode. The conflict between the light and darkness, the Christ-spirit and the self-spirit, may be long and arduous, but the issue is certain. Help, but do not hinder, the process. Be reverent, careful, mindful of the presence of God.

*Be hopeful for yourself.* When an art student asked Mr. Ruskin whether he would ever be able to paint like Turner, the great critic replied, "It is more likely that you will become Emperor of all the Russias!" But God never daunts a soul with such discouragement. He first sets before it a great ideal—the faith of Abraham, the meekness of Moses, the prayer of Elijah, the love of John—and then, as the source of all perfection, He enters the soul, to be in it all that He has taught it to desire.

*Count on the indwelling of His power.* The merchant of today has facilities granted to no previous age. The cablegram, telegram, and telephone put him in communication with the markets of the world; steam and electricity are his willing slaves in manufacture; machinery with its unwearying iron fingers toils for him. A single human brain, which knows how to avail itself of these resources, can multiply its conceptions indefinitely. How vast the space between the untutored savage, doing everything with his hands, and the merchant prince, who has but to press the ivory-plated buttons fixed on the walls of his room! But not less is the difference between the work we can accomplish by our natural resources, and that which we achieve when we recognize that what is impossible to us is possible to Him who has come in to abide. I cannot; but God is within me, and He can.

**The Conditions of the Divine Immanence**

*Love to Christ* "He that loveth me shall. . . ." We would love Him, but how? Do not think of your love, but of His. "Love is of God." Open the shutters of your being toward the love of God; we love because He first loved. Love is the reflection from us of what we have first received from God.

Love is shed abroad in the heart by the Holy Spirit. The fruit of the Spirit is love. Seek the infilling and inworking of the Spirit; be careful to obey His promptings to love; avoid grieving Him by bitterness, wrath, or evil speaking; sit as His willing pupil in the school of love; cast on Him the responsibility of securing in your nature obedience to the primal law, which is fulfilled in the one word, "Thou shalt love."

Beneath the nurturing grace of the Sprit, we shall be led to meditate much on the love of Jesus to us, especially as manifested in His on the cross; and as we muse, the fire will burn, love will glow, and afford the condition of soul that is infinitely attractive to the divine Lover, who requires our love, and produces the love that He requires.

*Obedience to Christ.* Where there is true love, there will be obedience. This rather than emotion. Many a sincere soul, who questions its love because its emotions are low or fluctuating, would rather die than disobey the least jot or tittle of His commandments. Such a one loves. "He that hath my commandments (treasured in memory and heart), he it is that loveth me." Why do ye call Him, Lord, Lord, and do not the things that He says? There may be the luscious language of the lip, but it does not deceive Him. He looks under the leaves for fruit.

Disobedience robs the soul of the sweet sense of Christ's indwelling. Nothing can compensate for failure to obey. Whatever the protestations, there is no real love to Christ where His commands are knowingly disregarded and set at nothing. But each time we dare to step out in simple obedience to His will, it seems as though the inner light shines deeper into the hidden places of our being, and the residence of Christ extends to new chambers of the heart.

# 13 Christ's Legacy and Gift of Peace

*Peace I leave with you, my peace I give unto you: not as the world giveth, give I unto you. Let not your heart be troubled, neither let it be afraid.*

*John 14:27*

It seems a little anomalous to talk of peace at a time when warclouds are always on the horizon, the sea roars, and men's hearts fail them for fear: and yet, in the deepest aspects, this is of all times the most suitable. It is when the storm rattles on the window panes that the family draws closer around the fire, and the mother clasps her babe to her breast.

The word "peace" is the Eastern salutation and benediction. When one stranger encounters another, as they meet and part they wish each other peace. It was befitting, therefore, that as Christ's entrance into our world the first salutation to men, as conveyed by the angels, should be "Peace on earth"; and that His parting words should be "Peace be unto you." But with what a wealth of meaning does the Lord invest familiar words when they issue from His lips! Let us draw nigh, and allow His sweet and soothing consolations to have their full effect.

**Let Us Distinguish Between "Peace" and "My Peace"**

"Peace I leave with you, my peace I give unto you." There is a distinction between these two. The former refers to the result of His work for us on the cross: "Being justified by faith, we have peace with God through our Lord Jesus Christ" (Rom. 5:1); the latter refers to *His* indwelling, who is our Peace. The one He has bequeathed as a *legacy* to all men: the Testator died, and left in His will a perfect reconciliation between God and man, which is for all who are willing to avail themselves of it; the other is *a gift*, which must be appropriated and used, or it will be ineffectual.

*The order of these two varieties of peace is invariable.* We must have peace *with* God before we can enjoy the peace *of* God. We must receive the Atonement, with all its blessed comfort, before we can enter upon our heritage in Christ Jesus. A believer, whose feet were dipping in the chill waters of the river, said to me recently, when speaking of her enjoyment of some of the deeper aspects of Christian experience, "I am afraid I have been building from the top. I see now, as I come near eternity, that one's foundations must be strong and sure before one can build on them. I need now more than ever the blood of Christ." This, perhaps, is one of the perils of the present day. The church is arraying herself in her beautiful garments. The gold pieces of Christian thought and life are becoming current coin; they are being taken from the coffers, where they have too long lain, and cast about. Treatises and tracts on the innermost aspects of the blessed life are as plentiful as flowers in May. There is a danger, therefore, of young converts and others occupying themselves with such themes, and not paying sufficient attention to the divine order.

Christ dying *for* us on the cross must precede Christ living *in* us by His Spirit; justification with its evidence must be well apprehended before sanctification with its fruits; the peace *with* God must shed its benediction over the soul before it can enter upon the peace *of* God. Ah, soul! you have experienced the former; do you know the latter? Do you know what it is for Christ to enter into the closed doors of the inner chamber of the heart, and say, "Peace be unto you"? Do you know what it is to hear His voice speaking above the tumult of the inland lake of your soul, and making a great calm? Do you know what it is for Him to deal with the springs of the inner life, which lie deeper than emotion or fancy, and pour in His infinite serenity, so that the outflow may be clear and tranquil?

Christ lays stress on *His* peace. He must mean the very peace that filled His own heart; not something like it, but the same, always keeping the heart with the affections, and the mind with its thoughts. This being so, we infer:

*That His peace is consistent with a perfect knowledge of coming sorrow.* He knew all things that awaited Him (John 18:4): the treachery of Judas, the denial by Peter, the forsaking by all, the shame and spitting, the cross and the grave; and yet He spoke serenely of His peace. It is therefore consistent with the certain outlook toward darkness and the shadow of death. You may know from certain symptoms that cancer has struck it fangs into your flesh, and that paralysis has begun to creep along your spine; that your dearest is barked by the Woodsman for felling; that your means of subsistence will inevitably dry up: but, facing all these, as Jesus faced the cross, you may still be conscious of a peace that passes understanding.

*That it is consistent with energetic action.* Men are disposed to think that peace is one of the last fruits of the tree of life that drop into the hand of the aged. A man says to himself, I shall have to relinquish this active life, to settle in some quiet country home in the midst of nature, and then perhaps I shall know what peace means. A snug home and a competence, the culture of flowers, the slow march of the seasons, tender home love far away from the hustling throng of the world—these are the conditions of peace. Not so, says Christ: "Arise, let us go hence." Let us leave this quiet harbor, and launch out into the stormy deep. Let us leave this still chamber, around the windows of which the vines cling, and go forth into the garden where the cedars fight with the tempest; and amidst it all we shall find it possible to enjoy the peace that passes knowledge. Let men and women immersed in the throng of daily toil, young men, busy men, understand that Christ's peace is for those who hear the bugle note of duty summoning them to arise and go from there.

*That the chief evidence of this peace is in the leisureliness of the heart.* Christ's possession of peace was very evident through all the stormy scenes that followed. With perfect composure He could heal the ear of Malchus, and stay the impetuosity of Peter; could reason quietly with the slave that smote Him, and bid the daughters of Jerusalem cease their weeping; could open Paradise to the dying thief, and the door of John's home to the reception of His mother. Few things betray the presence of His peace more than the absence of irritability, fretfulness, and feverish haste, which expend the adornments of life.

Oh that you may now receive from Christ this blessed gift! Let the peace of Christ rule in your heart; it is your high privilege, be not backward in availing yourself of it. It will be as oil to the machinery of life.

**The Sources of Christ's Peace**

*The vision of the Father*—"If ye loved me, ye would rejoice, because I said, I go unto the Father."

Throughout these closing chapters He seems able to speak of nothing else. His mind ranges from the disciples whom He was leaving to the Father to whom He was going. Almost unconsciously He gives us a glimpse of his self-repression in staying away from His Father's manifested presence so long, when He says that if we loved Him we would be glad to lose His bodily presence because He had gone to be with the Father. He gives us to understand how real and near the Father was to Him, and how He longed to be again in His bosom! He was so occupied with this thought, that He reckoned little of what lay between. Hail! ye stormy waters of death, stormy winds, and boisterous waves: ye do but waft my soul nearer its haven in the Father's love!

It is the thought of the Father that gives peace, because it robs life of its terrors and death of its sting. Why fear what life may bring, when the Father has arranged each successive step of its pathway! Why dread Judas or Caiaphas, Herod or Pilate, since the Father lies between them and the soul as a rampart of rock! Why lose heart amid the perplexities and discouragements whose dark shadows lie heavily on the hills, when in the green pastures of the valley the Father's love tends the sheep! Ask Christ to reveal the Father to you. Live in His everlasting love, and learn what He can be amid the storm and tumult as a very present help.

*Disentanglement from the world*—"The prince of this world cometh, and hath nothing in me." He came first at the beginning of the Savior's life, with temptations to his ambition; he came again at its close, with temptations to that natural shrinking from pain that is characteristic of a highly organized nature. "Back, Son of Man! Thou canst not bear the cross and spear, the nail and thorn! Thy tender flesh will ill sustain Thee when the sorrows of death and the pains of hell get hold upon Thee!" So Satan came; but there was no response in the heart of Christ, no answering voice from the depths of His soul, no traitor within to join hands with the tempter without. There was no square inch of territory in all Christ's nature that the devil could claim, or from which he could operate.

This is a clue to Christ's peace, which we do well to follow until it leads us out into the open. As long as we are entangled with this world, peace evades us—just as sleep, which comes easily to the laboring man who has nothing beyond his daily wage, vanishes from the pillow of the merchant, who on stormy nights thinks uneasily of the vessels that carry his wealth far out at sea. We must stand clear of the ambitions of the world, of the fear or favor of man, of the avaricious craving for wealth, or of the fear of poverty. We must put the cross of Christ between us and the world, which was judged at Calvary. We must be able to say truly that our treasure is in heaven, and our heart also; and that we seek the things where Christ sits at the right hand of God. Then the stock market may fluctuate; riches go or come; men praise or hate—nothing will affect our peace, any more than the tumults of a continental city, in which we are spending a night in transit, can cause us serious disturbance.

*Supreme love*—"I love the Father." I have often noticed how a supreme love in a young girl's life seems to calm and quiet her, because it draws the whole of her nature in one strong flow toward the man of her choice. Before that, there was a waywardness, a vacillation, a nervous excitement, which passed away as soon as love dawned on her soul. So long as the heart is subject to every influence, it quivers and wavers as the magnet needle when swept by streams of electricity. A strong uniting love does for us what the strong attraction of the pole does for the needle. Christ loved the Father. There was no difficulty in bearing what He sent, or doing what He bade. There were no rival claimants, no questionings or debate within the palace of His heart. Every passion and emotion was quieted and stilled in the set of His whole being toward the Father. If you too would have peace, you must love; you must love supremely Him who alone is worthy, who can never disappoint or fail. And in proportion as you love God, you will find pleasure in all beautiful things, in all lovely persons, in all the fair gifts of nature and life. Oh, love the Lord, O my soul, and all that is within me, love His holy name!

*A supreme source of authority*—"As the Father gave me commandment, even so I do." Every soul must have a supreme source of authority in its life, if it is to have peace. Its own whim, the suggestion of passion, the vagrant impulse of the moment are inconsistent with tranquility. There must be for each of us one voice that is imperative, one command that is indisputable, one authority that admits of no denial. If you will search your heart you will see that this is so. Compare the restlessness of the times of the Judges with the tranquility of the reign of Solomon, and you will have an apt illustration of your own experience before consecration put Christ on His throne, and afterward. When the true Melchisedec established His reign within you, at once your heart became Salem, the city of peace. When you put the government on His shoulder, He set up His reign within you as the Prince of Peace. Happily for you, if of the increase of His government there is no end; for of the increase of your peace there will be no end either.

Combine these four—the sense of God's presence and providence in the details of life; detachment from the world; a supreme love to God; the recognition in everything that you are His bondservant—and you will comply with the conditions of participating in the peace of Christ that He offers. Some persons have a marvelous faculty of imparting their own tranquility in an accident, a storm, an illness; their aspect, tones, manner, are like the repose of a summer's evening after a sultry day: so shall Christ be to you, and you to others.

**Christ's Giving Contrasted With the World's**

"Not as the world giveth, give I unto you."

The world wishes peace, but lightly speaks the word; frequently wishing it when there is least warrant for it; wishing it without doing anything to produce it; wishing it while glorying over a wrong, healing slightly a wound, covering with the turf the crater of a volcano. Christ, on the other hand, lays the foundations of peace in suitable conditions of a holy and healthy life.

With the world, peace is a passing emotion; with Christ, a settled principle of action—the perfect balance and equilibrium of the soul, out of which comes all that is fair, strong, wholesome.

The world's peace consists in the absence of untoward circumstances; Christ's is altogether independent of circumstances, and consists in the state of the heart. It matters nothing that in the world we have tribulation; He bids us be of good cheer, because in Him we shall have peace. The wildest conjunction of outward things cannot break the perfect peace of the soul that nestles to His heart, as Noah's dove to the hand that plucked it in from the weltering waters.

"Let not your heart be troubled," the Master says again. You may be troubled on every side; but be not troubled! Do not let the trouble come inside. Watch carefully against its intrusion, as you would against that of any other form of temptation. Let My peace, like a sentinel, keep you; and as you look forward to the unknown future, out of which spectral figures emerge, do not be afraid. There is a part for you to do, as well as for Me. I can give you My peace; but you must avoid any and everything that will militate against its possession and growth.

# 14 The Story of the Vine

*I am the true vine, and my Father is the husbandman.*
*John 15:1*

We have now a story to tell which, in the eye of heaven, will make our world forever memorable and wonderful among her sister spheres. It is the story of the vine, and how it was the divine purpose that our earth should be its fruitful soil, and our race intimately associated with its growth and history.

"I am the *true* vine," said our Lord. Not improbably, as He was walking with His disciples in the moonlit air, He perceived a vine clustering around the window or door; and with an eye ever awake to each touch of natural beauty, and a heart always alert for spiritual lessons, He turned to them and said, "What that vine is in the world of nature, I am in relation to all true and faithful souls. I am the *true* Vine"—true, not as opposed to false, but true in the sense of real, substantial, and enduring: the essential, as distinguished from the circumstantial; the eternal, as distinct from the temporary and transient.

Nature is a parable of God. In each of her forms we have a revelation of God—not so complete as that given through the mind of prophets, or the life of Jesus Christ; but still a revelation of the divine. Each natural object, as it stood in Eden's untainted beauty, displayed some aspect of Him whom no man can see and live. The apple tree among the trees of the wood; the rose of Sharon; the lily of the vale; the cedar, with its dark green foliage; the rock with its strength; the sea with its multitudinousness; the heaven with its limpid blue, like the divine compassion, overarching all—these are some of the forth-shadowings in the natural world of spiritual qualities in the nature of God. The vine was made the clinging, helpless plant it is, that it might forever remind men of certain deep characteristics of the divine nature.

**The Vine and Its Branches**

*The unity of the vine.* The vine and its branches constitute one plant. Some branches may be trailed along the trellis outside the cottage door, others conducted through hothouse after hothouse; yet one life, one stream of sap, one essential quality and character, pervades them all—from the dark root, buried in the soil, to the farthest twig or leaf. Yonder branch waving its fronds high up against the hothouse glass, cannot say to that long leafless branch hidden beneath the shelf, "You do not belong to me, nor I to you." No twig is independent of another twig. However different the functions, root and branches, leaves and cluster, all together make one composite but organic whole. So is it with Christ. All who are one with Him are one with each other. The branches that were nearest the root in the days of Pentecost are incomplete without the last converts that shall be added in the old age of the world. Those without these will not be made perfect.

This is the underlying truth of the holy Catholic Church. Men have tried to show that it must be an outward and visible organization, consisting of those who had received, through a long line of apostolical succession, some mystic power of administering rites and conferring absolution upon those who came beneath the touch of their priestly hands. That theory has notoriously broken down. But the truth of which it is a grotesque travesty is presented in our Lord's conception of the vine, deeply planted in the dark grave of Joseph's garden, which has reached down its branches through the ages, and in which every believing soul has a part. Touch Christ; become one with Him in living union; abide in Him—and you are one with the glorious company of the apostles, the goodly fellowship of the prophets, the noble army of martyrs, and the Church of the Firstborn, whose names are written in heaven.

*The pliancy of the vine.* More than most plants it needs a

husbandman. It cannot stand upright like other fruit trees; but requires a skillful hand to guide its pliant branches along the espaliers, or to entwine them in the trellis. It suggests a true thought of the appearance presented to the world by Christ and His church.

Mrs. Hamilton King, in her description of the sermon preached in the hospital by Ugo Bassi, on the eve of the great movement which, by the expulsion of the Austrians, gave Italy to the Italians, especially dwells on this. Down five wards the prisoners are living on the hospital beds from which they will never rise again. To them the deep voice of the hero-preacher tells the story of the vine: how "it is tied to a stake, and if its arms stretch out, it is but crosswise; they are also forced and bound."

Thus it was with Christ. Never following His own way, always bound to the imperative *must* of the Father's will, He yielded to the cross as a willing sufferer. And so it has been with His followers. Not strong to stand alone, but always yielded to the Father's will, that He should lead them where He would—to a cross, if needs be; to persecution and shame, if this would better serve His purpose; to a Gethsemane, if that were the only gate to life.

Yield yourself to those loving hands. They may lead you afar from your original purpose—twisting you in and out with many a contortion; fixing you with nail and fastening; trailing you over the wall, to droop your clusters to the hands of strangers. Nevertheless, be sure to let Him have His way with you; this is necessary for the accomplishment of His purpose.

*The suffering of the vine.* When, in the spring, "the grace of the green vine makes all the land lovely, and the shoots begin to wind and wave in the blue air," the husbandman comes in with pruning-hook and shears, and strips it bare of all its innocent pride. Nor is this all. Even in the vintage it is not allowed to glory in the results of the year; "the bunches are torn down and trodden in the wine-press, while the vine stands stripped and desolate."

So it has always been. The church has always, but at an infinite cost to herself, been instrumental in promoting the well-being of the world. Christ's people have always been a suffering people; and it is in exact proportion to their anguish that they have enriched mankind. They have saved others, but not themselves. The red stream of blood that has vitalized the world has flowed from broken hearts.

Measure thy life by loss instead of gain;
Not by the wine drunk, but by the wine poured forth:
For Love's strength standeth in Love's sacrifice,
And whoso suffers most hath most to give.

*The interdependence of vine and branches.* In God from eternity dwelled a wealth of love, pity, and yearning over the souls of men, that could not find direct expression. There was no language for the infinite passion of the divine heart. Hence the gift of the Son, through whom when He had become flesh, the Infinite might express Himself But even this was not sufficient. The vine root is not enough in itself; it must have branches to carry its rich juices to the clusters, so that these may hang free of each other in the sun and air. Christ must have branches—long lines of saved souls extending down the centuries—through which to communicate Himself to men.

We have seen how necessary the Vine is to the branches. Only from it can our fruit be found. But let us humbly, yet gladly, believe that we are also necessary to Christ. He cannot do without us. The Son wants sons; angels will not suffice. Through redeemed men alone can He achieve His eternal purpose. I hear the Vine pleading for more and yet more branch life, that it may cover the world with goodly shadow and fruit.

**Fruit or No Fruit?**

From all that has been said, it is clear that the one purpose in the vine is fruit-bearing. See here how the divine Teacher accentuates it: "fruit," "much fruit," "more fruit." Nothing less will content Him in any one of us. For this, we were taken out of the wild vine in which we were by nature, and grafted into Him; for this, the regeneration of the Holy Spirit, and the discipline of life; for this, the sunshine of His love, and the dew of the Holy Spirit. It becomes each seriously to ask, "Am I bringing forth fruit to God?" There may be orthodoxy of doctrine, correctness in life, and even heartiness of service; but is there fruit, much fruit, more fruit?

*Fruit!*—This is the only condition of being retained in living union with the Vine.

*Much fruit!*—Only thus will the Father be glorified.

*More fruit!*—Otherwise there must be the repeated use of the knife.

Nowhere does the Lord contemplate a *little fruit.* A berry here and there! A thin bunch of sour, unripened grapes! Yet it is too true that many believers yield no more than this. He comes to us hungry for grapes; but behold, a few mildewed bunches, not fit to eat!

Where there is *no fruit,* there has been no real union with the Vine. Probably you are a professor, but not a possessor; a nominal Christian, an attendant at church or chapel, but not really one with Christ. True union with Him produces a temper, a disposition, a ripe and mellow experience, which certainly indicate that Christ is within. You cannot stimulate the holy joy, the thoughtful love, the tranquil serenity, the strong self-control, which mark the soul that is in real union with Jesus; but where there is real abiding, these things will be in us and abound, and we shall be neither barren nor unfruitful in the knowledge of our Lord Jesus Christ.

**The Knife and the Fire**

"Every branch in me that beareth fruit," the Father, who is the Husbandman, "purgeth it, that it may bring forth more fruit." Too many children of God, when passing through great physical and other suffering, account it punishment. No, it is not punitive, but purgative. This is the pruning knife, cutting away the shoots of the self-life, that the whole energy of the soul may be directed to the manifesting of the life of the Lord Jesus. It may seem a grievous waste to see the floor of the hothouse or vineyard littered with fronds and shoots and leaves, but there need be no lament: the branches of the autumn will well repay each stroke of that sharp edge with fuller, richer fruit. So we gain by loss; we live as we die; the inward man is renewed as the outward decays.

The knife is in the Father's hand; let us never forget that.

He will not entrust this delicate and difficult work to man or angel. Shall we not be in subjection to the Father of our spirits and live? Blessed be the Father of our Lord Jesus, and our Father in Him. He who spared not Christ may be trusted to do the best for us.

Employing the same word, the Master said, Now you have been pruned through the word that I have spoken to you. Perhaps if we were more often to yield ourselves to the pruning of the Word, we would escape the pruning of sore pain and trial. If the work was done by the golden edge of Scripture, it might make the iron edge of chastisement needless. Therefore, when we take the Word of God in hand, let us ask the great Husbandman to use it for the pruning away of all that is carnal or evil, so that His life may have unhindered sway.

But if we will not bear fruit, we must be taken away. We shall lose our sphere of Christian service, and be exposed as hollow and lifeless professors. The vine branch that has no wealth of purple clusters is good for nothing. Salt which is savorless is fit neither for the land nor the dunghill. Vine branches that bear no fruit are cast into the fire. Professors that lack the grace of a holy temper, and the beauty of a consistent life, are taken away. "Men . . . cast them into the fire, and they are burned" (John 15:6).

These three years the divine Husbandman has come hungrily seeking fruit of you, yet in vain. Nevertheless, He will spare you for this year also, that you may mend your ways. This is the reason of your multiplied anxieties; He is pruning you. If you bear fruit, it will be well, eternally, well; but if not, then it is inevitable that you will be cut away as dead and useless wood.

# 15 *Abide in Me, and I in You*

*Abide in me, and I in you. As the branch cannot bear fruit of itself, except it abide in the vine; not more can ye, except ye abide in me.*

*John 15:4*

These words are so familiar by constant repetition, that their power to awaken the soul is greatly lessened. They go and come through ear and mind—as a lodger who has gone and come with exactly the same appearance and at precisely the same hours for years, and no one notices him now, because there is nothing novel about him to awake notice or remark. How good would it be if we could hear this tender injunction for the first time! Next to this, let us ask the divine Spirit to rid it of the familiarity of long use: to remint it, and to make it fresh and vital; that it may seem to us that we have never before realized how much Jesus meant when He said, *Abide in Me.*

Perhaps it may assist us if we adopt another English word for *abide*; and one which, in some respects even more closely, especially in sound, resembles the Greek. It is the word *remain*; so that we may read the Master's bidding thus: *Remain in Me, and I in you.*

This word is often employed in the New Testament in connection with house and home. "Mary abode [or remained] with Elisabeth for three months"; and, "There abide [or remain]," said our Lord, when giving His disciples directions for their preaching tour, and referring to some hospitable house that had been opened to welcome them. It is used three times in that memorable colloquy that introduced John and

Andrew to their future Teacher and Lord: "Master," they said, "where abidest [or remainest] thou? He saith unto them, Come, and ye shall see. They came therefore, and saw where he abode, and they abode with him that day." And again: "Zaccheus, make haste and come down, for to-day I must abide [or remain] in thy house." We are to remain in Christ as a man stays in his home.

*It is inferred, of course, that we are in Christ.* It would be absurd to bid a man remain in a house unless he were already within its doors. We must be sure that we are *in* Christ. Naturally we were outside—"Remember," says the apostle, "that aforetime ye were separate from Christ, alienated from the commonwealth of Israel, and strangers from the covenants of the promise, having no hope and without God in the world" (Eph. 2:12). We were shoots in the wild vine, partaking of its nature, involved in its curse, threatened by the ax that lay at its root. But all this is altered now. The Father, who is the Husbandman, of His abundant grace and mercy, has taken us out of the wild vine and grafted us into the true. "Of God are ye in Christ Jesus."

It is quite true that we repented of our sins, and turned toward God; that we have believed in Christ, and taken His yoke; that we have found rest under the shelter of His cross, and joy in expecting His advent: but we must never forget that behind all these movements of our will, and choice, and faith, were the willing and doing of God Himself. It is the Lord's doing, and it is marvelous in our eyes. "Blessed be the God and Father of our Lord Jesus Christ, who . . . hath begotten us again unto a [living] hope" (1 Peter 1:3). What confidence this gives us! We are in Christ by the act of God's grace and power; and surely He who put us in can keep us there. Did He not shut Noah into the ark, and keep him there amid all the crash of the pitiless deluge! We have only to consent to remain, and allow God to perfect that which concerns us. Be confident of this very thing, that He who began a good work in you will perform it until the day of Jesus Christ.

*The stress that the Master lays on our abiding in Him.* He appears to summon all His forces to accentuate His parting message. You always reserve your most important injunctions to the last, that they may remain fresh and impressive as the train steams out of the station, as the boat leaves the dock; so Christ left this entreaty to the last, that it might carry with it the emphasis of a parting message for evermore. But note how He drives it home. Its key word occurs eleven times in eleven consecutive verses. He depicts the terrible result if we do not abide: we shall wither, be taken away, and consigned to the fire. He shows how utterly we shall miss the one end of our existence—the glorification of the Father by fruit-bearing—unless we strenuously and continuously abide. He allures by the thought of the much fruit; by the assurance of success in prayer; by the promise of fullness of joy, of love, and of blessedness. He entreats, commands, exhorts, all in one breath. It is as though He were to say, "Children, I am leaving you: there are many things I desire for you, many commands to utter, many cautions, many lessons; but I am content to leave all unsaid, if only you will remember this one all-inclusive bidding—Abide in Me, remain in Me; stay where God has put you; deepen, emphasize, intensify, the union already existing between you and Me. From Me is your fruit found. Without Me you can do nothing. Abide in Me, and I in you. Grow up into Me in all things, which am the Head; rooted and built up in Me, and stablished by your faith, even as you were taught."

*There are many analogies to this appeal.* The sun says to the little planet earth, *Abide in me.* Resist the temptation to fly into space, remain in the solar sphere; and I will abide in the formation of your rocks, the verdure of your vegetation, and all living things, baptizing them in my fire.

*Abide in me,* says the ocean to the channel, that shows symptoms of division from its waves. Keep your channel unsilted and open, and twice in every twenty-four hours I will pour my fullness up to your farthest shore.

*Abide in me:* the vine says it to the branch, that it may impart supplies of life and fruit; the air says it to the lung, that it may administer ozone and oxygen to its cells; the magnet says it to the needle, that it may communicate its own specific quality, and fit it to guide across the ocean the mighty steamer, laden with the freight of human life.

*Abide in me:* the artist says it to the novice; Edison would say it to some young Faraday; the preacher to the student. Any man who is eager to impart his ideas to coming time is glad when some young life, eager, quick to receive formative impressions, presents itself. Here, says he, is my opportunity of incarnating myself afresh, and still living, speaking, painting, when my life is done. "Stay with me, young soul; share my home; saturate yourself with my ideas and methods of expression; go to no other fields to glean—and I will give my best self in return."

So, also, the mother speaks to the child. If she is wise, she will resist handing it over to the nurse, or sending it away to the care of strangers, except for the hours necessary for education. The child will bring companions and games, books and studies, within the influences of her love; and she, in return, will gladly bestow herself to the eager life that waits on her every movement, look, and word.

In all these cases, it is always the stronger that pleads with the weaker to abide, promising the communication of fuller life. Each, in measure, says, in the words of the glorious Christ, "I am stronger, wiser, fuller, better, than you. All is Mine that it may be yours: therefore, abide in Me, and I will abide in you."

*Notice Christ's consciousness of sufficiency for the needs of men.* It was blasphemous audacity to speak this way, if He were not more than man. He affirms that there can be no life apart from Him; that souls not united with Him wither on the forest floor. He says that fruitbearing is possible only to those who receive from His fullness grace for grace. He says that to be in union with Him will secure union with all holy souls. He says that if His words are carefully pondered and obeyed, we shall make no petition which His Father will not grant. He says that His love, in quality and quantity, is like the love that God has toward Himself; that His commands take rank with those of diety. He offers Himself to all mankind in coming ages, as their contemporary, and as the one sufficient source of life and godliness. All these assumptions are made in the range of these verses; and as we ponder them, we feel that the Speaker must be conscious of being other than human, and as possessing those infinite attributes that are the sole property of the Eternal.

Yet who shall say that He has offered more than He can give? Have we not tested Him in each of these particulars, and do not we, who have come to Him by faith, know that in no one item has He been guilty of exaggeration? We were dead; but behold, we live! We spent our energies in profitless work; but now we bear fruit to God. We were lonely and isolated; but now have come to the heavenly Jerusalem, to the innumerable company of angels, and to the church of the first-born. Our prayers were aimless and ineffective, but now we have the petitions we desired. New hope and joy have filled our hearts—as the ruddy clusters hang full and ripe in the autumn. Prove Him for yourself, and see if this shall not be so for you also. Only give yourself entirely up to Christ. Abide in Him. Remain in Him. Let thought and speech and life be bathed in the influences of His Holy Spirit; let the sap of His life flow where the sap of the self-life was wont to flow; and lo! old things will pass away, and all things will become new.

*The law and method of abiding.* There are two currents always flowing within our reach:

The "Not I," and the "I."

The last Adam, and the first.

The Spirit, and the flesh.

God has put us by His grace into the first of these. The Master says, "Stop there." It is much as when a father puts his little boy on the train, *en route* home, and says, "My boy, stop where you are. Do not get out; no change is necessary." We are in Christ by regeneration and faith. We may not always be thinking about Him, but we remain in Him, unless by unfaithfulness or sin we consciously and voluntarily leave Him. And if we have left Him for a single moment, it is always possible by confession and renewal to regain our old position.

This is confessedly an inadequate figure of speech. There is a sense in which the member cannot be amputated from the body, and the soul cannot be divorced from its union with Christ. But we are not dealing now with our integral oneness with Christ for life, but with our abiding union with Him for fruit bearing and service. And again we say, for those who are so immersed in daily business as to be unable for long to keep their minds fixed on Christ, that their abiding in Him does not depend on their perpetual realization and consciousness of His presence, but on the faith that they have done and said nothing inconsistent with the holy bond of fellowship.

You are in an elevator until you step out of it, though you may not be thinking of the elevator. You keep on a road until you take a turn right or left, although, engrossed in conversation with your friend, you do not think of the road. You are in Christ, amid the pressure of daily care, and the haste of business, so long as your face is toward the Lord, your attitude that of humble submission, and your conscience void of offense. During the day it is therefore possible at any moment to say, "I am in Thee, O blessed Christ. I do not have all the rapture and passion of more radiant hours; but I am in Thee, because I would not by a single act leave Thy secret place." If at such a moment you are conscious that you are not able to say as much, instantly go back over the past few hours, discover the place where you severed yourself from your Lord, and return.

Study Godet's beautiful definition of abiding: "It is the continuous act by which the Christian lays aside all he might draw from his own wisdom, strength and merit, to desire all from Christ by the inward aspiration of faith."

When, therefore, temptation arises to leave the words of Christ (v. 7) for the maxims of the world, step back, remain in Him, deny yourself.

Whenever you are tempted to leave the narrow path of His commandments (v. 10) to follow the impulses of your own nature, consider yourself dead to these, that you may run in those.

Whenever you are tempted to forsake the holy temper of Christ's love, for jealousy, envy, hatred—step back and say, I will not go out of my hiding place; I elect to remain in the love of God. The one effort of life is therefore reduced to a persistent resistance of all the suggestions of the world, the flesh, and the devil, that we should step out of that blessed Man into whom the Father has grafted us. Then He abides in us. He is strong where we are weak; loving and tender where we are thoughtless; holy where we fail. He is in us as wisdom, righteousness, sanctification, and redemption; and as the hope of glory.

# 16 *Prayer That Prevails*

*If ye abide in me, and my words abide in you, ye shall ask what ye will, and it shall be done unto you.*

*John 15:7*

Christ expected answers to His prayers; and in all His teaching leads us to feel that we shall be able to obtain, through prayer, what otherwise would not come to us. He knew all that was to be known of natural law and the Father's heart; but, notwithstanding His perfect acquaintance with the mysteries of the Father's government, He said, "Ask what ye will, and it shall be done unto you."

A careful comparison of the confident assurances of the Master and the experience of Christians as detailed in their biographies or personal confessions, discloses a wide difference between His words and the findings of His disciples. Many have become accustomed to disappointment in prayer. They have asked so many things that they have never received; have sought so much without finding: have knocked so repeatedly, but the door has remained closed. We are in the habit of accounting for our failure by saying that our prayer probably was not according to the will of God, or that God withheld the less that He might give us something better. In some cases there may be even an unspoken misgiving about the harmony of prayer with our Father's love and wisdom, or with a perfect confidence in Him as doing the best for us in the world. We forget that if we prayed as we should, we should ask what was according to His will. We evade Christ's definite words, "*Whatsoever* ye shall ask in my name, that will I do" (John 14:13).

When we consider the lives of some who have done mighty things for God, it is clear that they had learned a secret that eludes many of us. Take this, for instance, from the biography of Dr. Burns Thomson. "When much together as students," writes his friend, "we agreed on special petitions, and the Lord encouraged us by giving answers, so early and so definite, as could only have come from Himself; so that no room was left for the shadow of a doubt that God was the Hearer and Answerer of prayer. Once the answer came the same day, and at another time, whilst we were yet speaking. My friend often spoke of our agreement, to the glory of Him who fulfilled to us his promise; and I refer to it to encourage others." This is but one leaf out of the great library of prayers, intercessions, and supplications for all saints, which stand recorded before God.

We naturally turn to our Lord's last utterances, in which His instructions about prevailing prayer are fuller than those of the Sermon on the Mount; and than those given in the midst of His earthly life, which depict the importunity of the widow with the unjust judge, and of the friend with his friend at midnight. The words spoken in the chapter we are now considering are particularly pertinent to our purpose, because they deal exclusively with the age to which our Lord frequently referred as "that day"—the Day of Pentecost, the age of the Holy Spirit, the day of this dispensation.

**Our Lord Teaches That Any Prayer That Is to Prevail With God Must Pass Five Tests**

These are but different phases of the same attitude.

*The glory of the Father.* "That the Father may be glorified in the Son" (John 14:13). The one purpose of Christ on earth was to glorify the Father; and at the close of His life here He was conscious that He had not striven in vain. "Now," He said, "is the Son of man glorified, and God is glorified in him" (John 13:31). This was the purpose of His earthly career, and it was perfectly consistent with that of His eternal being; for each person of the Holy Trinity is ever intent on unfolding and displaying the moral beauty of the other two. Having sat down at the right hand of the Majesty on high, Christ still pursues His cherished purpose of making His Father known, loved, and adored. No prayer, therefore, can hope to succeed with Him, or can claim His concurrent intercession, which is out of harmony with this sublime intent.

Whatever petition we offer should be submitted to this standard—Can we establish it in the presence of Christ, that our request will promote the glory of the Father? Bring in your evidence—establish your pleas—adduce your strong reasons. If you can make good your claim, your prayer is already granted. But be sure that it is impossible to seek the glory of God consistently with selfish aims. These two can no more coexist than light and darkness in the same cubic space. The glory of God will ever triumph at our cost. It is equally certain that none of us can truly pray for the glory of God, unless we are living for it. It is only out of the heart that has but one purpose in life and death that those prayers emanate which touch the tenderest chord in the Savior's nature, and awaken all His energies to their highest activity: "That will I do."

*In Christ's Name.* "Whatsoever ye shall ask in my name" (John 14:13). Throughout the Holy Scriptures, *name* stands for *nature.* The Master says, "You must ask in My nature." In other words, when we pray, it must not be as the self nature, but as the Christian nature, dictates. We always know when that is paramount. It excludes boasting; it is pure, peaceable, and loving; it is far removed from the glare and gaudiness of the world; it is full of Calvary, Olivet, and Pentecost. There are days in our life when we feel borne along on its tidal current. When Christ is in us, the hope of glory; when a power is working within us beyond what we can ask or think; when we live, yet not we, but Christ in us—these are the times most propitious for prayer. Pour out your heart before God. Let the Christ nature, which is in you by the Holy Spirit, speak to Christ on the throne. Let the living water, which has descended from the eternal city, return to its source through the channel of your heart. This is praying in His name, and according to His nature.

Before we can expect our prayers to prosper, let us sit down quietly, and, putting aside all other voices, permit the Christ nature to speak. It is only in proportion as it countersigns our petitions that they will reach the audience chamber of eternity. Surely, if this test were properly applied, many of the petitions we now offer so glibly would never leave our lips; and we would be satisfied about the fate of many other prayers which, like some ill-fated ship, has left our shores, and never been heard of again. But again let it be remembered that none can pray in the name of Christ who do not live for that name—like those early evangelists of whom John says that for the sake of the name they took nothing of the Gentiles. The name of Christ must be predominant in life, if it is to be efficacious in prayer.

*Abide in Christ.* "If ye abide in me . . . ask what ye will" (John 15:7). We are in Christ by the grafting of the great Husbandman, who took us out of the wild vine of nature, and incorporated us with Christ. That union is forever; but its conscious enjoyment and helpfulness arise only insofar as we keep His commandments. A limb may be in the body, and yet be dislocated and useless. If you are in a train traveling to your destination at the terminus, all that is necessary is to resist the temptation to alight at the stations *en route,* and to remain where you are. If, then, God the Father has put you into Christ, and is seeking to establish you in Him, be careful to resist every temptation or suggestion to depart from living fellowship by any act of disobedience or unbelief.

If you abide in Christ in daily fellowship, it will not be difficult to pray aright, for He has promised to abide in those who abide in Him; and the sap of the Holy Spirit, securing for you fellowship with your unseen Lord, will produce in you, as fruit, desires and petitions similar to those that He unceasingly presents to His Father. Throughout the ages Christ has been asking of God. This is the perpetual attitude of the Son to the Father. He cannot ask what the Father may not give. To get then into the current of His prayer is to be sure of success. Abide in Him, that He may abide in you; not only in the activities of holy service, but in the intercessions and supplications of the hour of private prayer.

*Submit prayer to the correction of the Word.* "If my words

abide in you" . . . (John 15:7). Christ's words have been compared to a court of solemn and stately personages, sitting to try our prayers before they pass on into the Master's presence.

Here is a prayer that is selfish and earth-born, grasping at the prizes of worldly ambition and greed. But as it enters it encounters that solemn word, "*Seek ye first the kingdom of God and his righteousness*" (Matt. 6:33), and it turns back surprised and ashamed.

Here is another prayer, full of imprecation and unkindness toward someone who has maligned or injured the petitioner. But it is met by that solemn word of the Master, "*Love your enemies . . . pray for them that despitefully use you*" (Matt: 5:44), and it hastens to retire.

Here is another prayer full of murmuring regret because of the pressure of the cross, the weight of the restraining yoke. But that notable word of Christ forbids its further progress, saying, "*In the world ye shall have tribulation: but be of good cheer; I have overcome the world*" (John 16:33). In the presence of that reminder and rebuke, the prayer, abashed, turns away its face and departs. Like the accusers of the woman taken in the act of sin, prayers like these are inwardly convicted of unfitness, and go forth.

The words of Christ forbid unsuitable prayer; but they also stir the heart with great desire for the realization of those good things that Christ has promised to those who love Him. In this sense prayer becomes a dialogue between the Master who says, "Seek ye my face," and the disciple who responds, "Thy face, Lord, will I seek."

*Fruit-bearing.* "I appointed you . . . that ye should go and bear fruit that . . ." (John 15:16). In other words, answers to prayer depend largely on our ministry to others. If we are prompted by desire for our own comfort, peace, or enjoyment, we shall stand but a poor chance of audience in the secret of His presence. If, on the other hand, our prayers are connected with our fruit-bearing—that is, with our ministry to others, with the coming of the kingdom, and the accomplishment of God's purpose of salvation—the golden scepter will be extended to us, as when Ahasuerus said to Esther, "What is thy request?

even to the half of the kingdom it shall be performed" (Esth. 5:6).

Is sun needed to ripen the fruit? Ask for it. The Father waits to give it. Is dew or rain needed that the pitchers may be filled to the brim with water that is to be made wine? Ask for it. God is not unrighteous to forget your work and labor of love. Ask for all but pruning; this the Father will administer, according to the good pleasure of His goodness. The fruit-bearing branches have a right to claim and appropriate all that is needed for the sweetening and ripening of their precious burden.

The temple of prayer is thus guarded from the intrusion of the unprepared footstep by many tests. At the foot of the marble steps we are challenged for the watchword; and if we do not speak in harmony with God's glory our further passage is peremptorily stayed. The key, engraved with the name of Jesus, will only obey the hand in which His nature is throbbing. We must be in Him, if He is to plead in us. His words must prune, direct, and control our aspirations; His service must engage our energies. We must take part in the camp with His soldiers, in the vineyard with His husbandmen, in the temple building with His artificers. It is as we serve our King that we can count absolutely on His answer to our prayers.

**Three Concluding Thoughts Remain**

*First.* It is clear that our prayers depend largely on our inner life. Where that is vigorous and healthy, they will be the same. But let deterioration and failure set in, and the effect will be instantly apparent in our prayers. Out of the abundance of the heart the mouth speaks; and when the mouth is opened in prayer and supplication, the heart speaks.

*Second.* Bespeak the Spirit's indwelling. He is the bond of communion and fellowship between the Father and the Son, and will lift us into the holy circle of that eternal life, so that the current may pass through us with uninterrupted velocity and force. He makes inward intercession for the saints according to the will and mind of God.

*Third.* Expect that prayer will become ever more engrossing, as the divine impulse is yielded to; so that what now occupies but a comparatively small portion of time and energy will become with us, as with the great aspostle, an exercise which we prosecute with unceasing ardor, an ever-delightful method of promoting the Redeemer's kingdom.

# 17 The Hatred of the World

*They shall put you out of the synagogues: yea, the time cometh, that whosoever killeth you will think that he doeth God service. And these things will they do unto you, because they have not known the Father, nor me.*

*John 16:2, 3*

How near love and hate dwell in these words of Jesus! He had been urging His disciples to cultivate perfect love, the love of God; He now turns to describe the inevitable hatred with which they would be assailed in the world that knew neither the Father nor Himself. And if an additional motive were needed to induce that love, it would surely be given by the consideration of that hate.

This is no unimportant theme. It touches very nearly the lives of thousands of believers among us. Though they do not have to face the thumbscrew and the stake, they discover painfully enough that the offense of the cross has not ceased. There are among us many who daily quiver under the venomous gibe of neighbor and fellow-worker, and find that their acceptance of Jesus Christ as Savior and Master has suddenly changed their family life and their working life from a garden of roses into a bed of thorns. Many a young person in the office, many a mechanic at the bench, many a traveler on the trains or planes, many a student on the college campus is doomed to discover that the world does not love the church better than in those days when the fires gleamed in Smithfield, and men and women were burned to death for loving God. But how sweet to know that all this verifies the Master's words: "[Ye] are not of the world, even as I am not of the world.

If ye were of the world, the world would love his own: but because ye are not of the world, but I have chosen you out of the world, therefore the world hateth you" (John 17:16; 15:19).

**What, Then, Is "the World"?** It consists of those who are destitute of the life and love of God, as contrasted with those who have received and welcomed the unspeakable gift that is offered to all in Jesus Christ. The great mass of the unregenerate and unbelieving, considered as a unity, is "the world," as that term is sometimes distinctively used by Christ and His apostles.

The world has its god; its religion, which was first instituted by Cain at the gates of Eden; its prince, and court, and laws; it maxims and principles; its literature and pleasures. It is dominated by a peculiar spirit that the apostle calls a lust or fashion, and resembles the German *Zeit-Geist*: an infection, an influence, a pageantry, a witchery; reminding us of the fabled mountain of loadstone that attracted vessels to itself for the iron that was in them, and presently drew the nails from the timbers, so that the whole fabric fell a helpless, shapeless mass into the waves. The votaries of the world attach themselves to the objects of sense, to the things that are seen and temporal. They have the utmost horror of poverty, suffering, and humiliation; these they consider their chief evils, to be avoided at any cost; while they regard as the chief good, riches, pleasure, and honor.

The world is thus a great unity and entity; standing together as a mighty kingdom; united and compacted together as Nebuchadnezzar's image; environing the church, as the great kingdoms of Assyria and Egypt did the chosen people of God in the days of the kings. It resembles a pack of wolves. "Behold," said Christ, "I send you forth as sheep in the midst of wolves" (Matt. 10:16). Between such irreconcilable opposites as the church and the world, there cannot but be antagonism and strife. Each treasures and seeks what the other rejects as worthless. Each is devoted to ends that are inimical to the dearest interests of the other. Each follows a prince, who met the prince of the other in mortal conflict. Let us thank Him who out of this world chose us for Himself.

**Let Us Trace Story of the World's Hatred**

*It was foretold in Eden.* "I will put enmity," so God spoke to the serpent, "between thee and the woman, and between thy seed and her seed" (Gen. 3:15). We are not disposed to treat that ancient record with which our Bible opens as romance or fairy tale; but to regard it as containing a true and authentic record of what actually transpired. That declaration is the key to the Bible. On every page we meet the conflict, the bruising of the church's heel by the dark powers, and the increasing area of victory covered by our Emmanuel, the virgin's Child. This hatred is then in the very nature of things, for this is but another name for God. It is, like others of the deepest facts in the experience of man, fundamental and inevitable, the outcome of mysteries that lie beyond the ken of man.

*And it has characterized every age.* Abel is slain by Cain, who was of the evil one, and slew his brother, Joseph is put into a pit by his brethen, and into a prison by his master's wife; the Hebrew is smitten by the Egyptian; David is hunted by Saul as a partridge on the mountains; Micaiah is hated by Ahab because he always testifies against him; Jeremiah lives a very suffering stricken life, until he is slain in Egypt for remonstrating against a policy he could not alter; each of the little company then listening to Christ is forecast for a martyr's death, with, perhaps, the exception of John himself, whose life was martyrdom enough; Stephen sheds the blood of his pure and noble nature; and from that day to this the blood of the saints has poured in streams.

Each age has had its martyr roll. They have been tortured, not accepting deliverance; have had trial of mockings and scourgings, yea, moreover of bonds and imprisonment; have been stoned, sawed in two, tempted, and slain with the sword; wandering in deserts and mountains and caves and the holes of the earth: of whom the world was not worthy.

*The root or ground of hatred is not due to the evil discovered in the persons who are the objects of the world's hate.* "They hated me without a cause" (John 15:25), our Savior sorrowfully said. There might have been some cloak for the shamelessness of the world's sin, if He had not spoken words and done works among them such as none other ever said and did; but in the face of the perfect beauty of His character, the grace and truth of His words, and the loveliness of His deeds, it was by their treachery He was crucified and slain. In vain He challenged them to convict Him of sin, and to bear witness to any evil that might justify their malicious cruelty. They knew it was innocent blood; but this knowledge, so far from mollifying them, only exasperated them the more.

The world hates the church, not for the evil that is in it, but for the good. It hates without cause. The holier and purer a life is, the more certainly it will attract to itself malignity and dislike. The more Christlike we are, the more we must suffer the relentless hate that drove the nails into His hands, and the spear into His side. Do not be surprised at this. Think it not strange concerning the fiery trial which comes to prove you, as though a strange thing happened to you; but doubt and question and be in fear, if you meet only smiles and flattery and such honors as the world can give. You may then ask yourselves whether you are not one of the world's own.

*The real origin and fountain of the hatred of the world is due to Satan's antagonism to God.* In his original creation, he was doubtless as fair as any of the firstborn sons of light; but in his pride he substituted himself for God, and love faded out of his being, making way for the unutterable darkness of diabolic hate. Satan hates God with a hatred for which there are no words; and therefore when the Father sent the Son to be the Savior of the world, Satan gathered up every energy and resource of his nature to dog his steps, and make his course through the world as painful as possible. Do you wonder that the life of Jesus was so full of suffering? It could not have been otherwise. God, in the person of Jesus, directly stepped down into the timesphere, and assumed the conditions of earth and death, He came within the range of the utmost that Satan could do to molest and injure Him. Similarly, when the blessed Lord becomes the tenant of the heart, and in proportion as He is so, that heart attracts to itself the hatred with which the devil from the beginning has hated God. "If they have persecuted me, they will also persecute you; if they have kept my saying, they will keep yours also. But all these things will they do unto you for my name's sake, because they know not him that sent me" (John 15:20-21).

*It is natural for the evil to hate the good.* First, the sinner has an uneasy conscience, and it hurts him to come in contact with those whose character reminds him of what he ought to be, and might be, and perhaps once was. The diseased eye dreads the light. The uncanny, slimy things that lurk beneath stones, and in dark caves, squirm in pain when you let in the day. The Turkish Sultan disliked the presence of British representatives, and correspondents of the Daily Press, amid the dark deeds of blood and lust by which he made Armenia a desert. "Every one that doeth evil hateth the light, neither cometh to the light, lest his deeds should be reproved" (John 3:20).

In addition to an uneasy conscience, the sinner has an unbroken will. He stoutly resists the impression of a superior and condemning goodness. He hardens his heart, and strengthens its defenses. "Who is the Lord, that I should obey his voice? Double the tale of bricks: summon the choice chariots and veteran soldiers of Egypt, that we may pursue, overtake, and divide the spoil." Such are the successive boasts and challenges of the hardened heart.

Is it to be wondered at, under such conditions, that the wicked plots against the just, and gnashes on him with his teeth; that he draws his sword and bends his bow, to shoot at the upright of heart? "The wicked watcheth the righteous, and seeketh to slay him. The Lord will not leave him in his hand, nor condemn him when he is judged" (Ps. 37:32-33).

*The great object of this hatred is to overcome the good.* In this respect the hate of the world is like the love of the church. The child of God loves, that he may overcome the evil in the world, by converting evildoers from the error of their ways and assimilating them to holiness; the child of the devil hates, that he may overcome the good of the world, by arresting their goodness, and assimilating them to evil. Ah, how thankful we may be that we are not of the world, but have been chosen out of it; for it lies in the wicked one, and is infected with the hatred of hell.

It is not difficult, therefore, to go through the world, and escape its hate. We have only to adopt its maxims, speak its language, and conform to its ways. In a well-known picture, the young girl, with pleading, upturned face, seeks to tie the Royalist scarf around the arm of her Huguenot lover. She will secure his safety if she succeeds! Ah, how many pleading glances are cast at us to induce us to spare ourselves and others, by toning down our speech, and covering our regimentals by the disguising cloak of conformity to the world around! "If you do not approve, at least you need not express your disapproval." "If you cannot vote for, at least do not vote against." "If you dissent, put your sentiments in courtly phrase, and so tone them down that they may not offend sensitive ears." Such is the advice that is freely proffered. But those who follow it quickly discover that the compromise of principle involves certainly and awfully the loss of influence for good.

**Our Behavior Amid the World's Hatred.** We have fallen on evil days. The world has been coated over with a Christian veneer, while the church has become leavened with the subtle spirit of the world. It is hard to come out and be separate, because in the dim twilight one is apt to mistake friend and foe. The bribes are so rich for those who conform, the dissuasives so strong for those who refuse to bow to the great golden image. But our duty is clear. We must be true to the Spirit of Christ. We must live a holy and unworldly life; we must avoid all that might be construed as an unworthy compromise of the interests of our Master's kingdom.

And through all the pitiless storm of hate that beats in our faces, we must be glad. "Blessed are ye," said our Lord, "when men shall revile you, and persecute you, and shall say all manner of evil against you falsely, for my sake. Rejoice, and be exceeding glad" (Matt. 5:11-12). And why rejoice? Because your reward is great in heaven; because you know that you are not of the world; because you are shown to be on the path trodden by the saints before you, every step of which has been trodden amid similar manifestations of the devil's hate.

Moreover, abound in love. Let there be no slackening of the

patient, tender, pitying love that heaps coals of fire on the head of the wrongdoer, and will never rest content until it has subdued the evil of his heart, overcoming it with good. Love must ultimately conquer hate, as surely as tomorrow's sun will conquer the darkness that now veils the landscape.

# 18 The Work of the Holy Spirit on the World

*He will reprove the world of sin, and of righteousness, and of judgment.*

*John 16:8*

Three facts forced themselves home on the apostles while listening to the Lord's parting words. *First,* that they were to be bereaved of their Master's presence (v. 5). *Second,* that they were to be left alone, amid the world's hatred—"Whosoever killeth you" (v. 2). *Third,* that their mission would be witness-bearing to the unseen Lord (15:27).

And as they fully realized all that these facts involved, they became too absorbed in their own sorrowful conclusions to inquire what realm the Master sought as He set sail from these earthly shores. "O Master," they said in effect, "why can You not stay? Our orphaned hearts will never be able to endure the blank which your absence will cause. Easier could a flock of sheep withstand the onset of a pack of wolves than we the hatred of the world! And as for our witness-bearing, it will be too feeble to avail anything."

And the Master, in effect, answered: "I will not leave you without aid. I shall still be with you, though unseen. My presence shall be revealed to your spirits, and made livingly real through the Blessed Comforter. He will be with you, and in you. He will authenticate and corroborate your witness. He will testify of Me; and when He is come, He will convince the world of sin, of righteousness, and of judgment. You see then that I shall be able to help you better by sending the Holy Spirit than by staying with you Myself. It is expedient for *you* that I go away; for if I do not go away the Comforter will not come to you, but if I depart I will send Him to you."

We may not be able to fathom all the reasons for Christ's withdrawal before the Spirit's advent was possible. But some of them are obvious enough. The full union of the Son of God with our race must be secured through death and resurrection; and His full union with the Father must be indicated in His glorification with the glory He had before the worlds were made—before He could be the perfect channel of communicating the divine fullness to our human nature. The Head must be anointed before the body. There must be no physical distraction arising from the outward life of Jesus to compete with the spiritual impression of His unseen presence. The text must be completed before the sermon can be preached. Christ must die, or there can be no witness to His atonement; must rise, or there can be no testimony to His resurrection; must ascend, or there can be no declaration as to His finished work and eternal intercession. Since the Spirit reveals Christ, all that was appointed to Christ to do must be completed before the Spirit can begin his ministry.

The work of the Spirit on the world is through the church, and is described by our Lord as threefold. By His revelation of Christ He creates three convictions. Each of these is necessary to the regeneration of man. There must be the sense of sin, or he will not seek the Savior. There must be a belief that righteousness is possible, or the convicted sinner will die of despair. There must be the assurance that sin is doomed, and shall be finally vanquished, or the baffled warrior will give up the long conflict as hopeless.

**The Conviction of Sin**

We are constantly meeting people who are perfectly indifferent to Christianity, because they say they do not feel their need of it. Why should they trouble about it, when they suppose themselves able to do perfectly well without it?

In dealing with these, it is a great mistake to entice them toward the gospel by describing the moral grandeur of Christ's character and teaching. We should at once seek to arouse them to a sense of their great sinfulness. When a man realizes that his life is being eaten out by some insidious disease, he will need no further urging to go to a physician. This is the weakness of much modern preaching—that we expatiate on the value of the remedy to men who have never realized their dire necessity.

But what is the truth most appropriate for producing the conviction of sin in the human breast? "Preach the Ten Commandments in all their stern and uncompromising 'shalts' and 'shalt-nots,' " cries one. "Read the descriptions given in Scripture of the evil things that lurk in the heart of man as filthy things in darksome caves," says another. "Show men the results of sin, take them to the edge of the bottomless pit," insists a third. But not one of these is the chosen weapon of the Holy Spirit. He convicts men of the sin of refusing to believe in Jesus Christ.

There stands the cross, the evidence and symbol of God's love; and there stands the risen Christ, offering Himself to men. There is nothing that more certainly proves the innate evil of the human heart than its refusal of that mystery of grace. Disbelief is the creature, not of the intellect, but of the will. It is not the result of inability to understand, but of stubborn obstinacy and stiffneckedness. Here is the supreme manifestation of moral beauty; but man has no eyes for it. Here is the highest revelation of God's desire for man to be reconciled to Him, and be at one with Him, as His happy child; but man either despises or spurns His overtures. Here is the offer of pardon for all the past, of heirship of all the promises, of blessedness in all the future; but man admits that he is indifferent to the existence and claims of God, and is quite willing to accept the sleeping retribution of bygone years, and to risk a future irradiated by no star of hope. Here is God in Christ beseeching him to be reconciled, declaring how much the reconciliation has cost; but the frail child of yesterday absolutely refuses to be at peace. No trace of tears in his voice, no shame on his face, no response to God's love in his heart.

This is sin at its worst. Not in a Nero drenched with the blood of relatives and saints; nor in an Alva expert to invent new methods of torture; nor in the brutalized expression of the felon; nor in the degradation of the heathen: but in those beside you, who have heard of the love of Jesus from their earliest childhood, and who know that He died for them, and waits to bless them, but who deliberately and persistently refuse Him—you will find the most terrible revelation of what man is capable of. "This is the condemnation, that light is come into the world, and men loved darkness rather than light, because their deeds were evil" (John 3:19).

Conviction in itself is not enough. Many have been convicted who have never gone on to conversion, resembling untimely fruit, which, blighted before its maturity, has dropped to the ground.

Conviction of sin does not come to all in the same manner or to the same extent. Indeed, those who have come to Christ in early life are in a degree exempt from drinking this bitter cup, though they have much tenderness of conscience afterward.

Do not wait for more conviction, but come to Jesus as you are, and tell Him that the saddest symptom in your case is your inability to feel as you know you should. Do not wait to be convinced of sin. Do not stay away until you feel more deeply. Do not suppose that strongly roused emotions purchase His favor. His command is absolute—*Believe*! But whenever that true repentance is wrought that needs not to be repented of, or those tears of penitence fall from the eyes of the suppliant, the means will always be the person and work and love of Jesus Christ. This is the glass through which the Spirit focuses the rays of God's love on ice-bound hearts.

**The Conviction of Righteousness**

The aggravation of sin of which the Spirit convicts the sinner seems to present a gloom too dark for any ray to penetrate. He cannot forget. The dead past will not bury its dead. The wind of eternity blows away the leaves with which he tries to hide the corpses of murdered opportunities, broken hearts, and dissipated years. He cannot forget. He may close his eyes, but still the memories of the past will haunt him—the deeds he would undo, the words he would recall, the dark ingratitude toward the love of Jesus. Conscience is a flaming terror until a man finds Christ as his Savior. Her brow is girded with fire, her voice peals with doom.

"Can I ever be cleansed?" cries the convicted soul. "Can these awful gnawings be ended, and these terrors laid to rest? Can I rise from this ruin and become a new, righteous, God-like man?" These questions are answered by the Spirit who induced them. "There is righteousness," He says, "because Christ is gone to the Father, and you see Him no more."

He is gone to the Father; and the seal of divine authenticity has therefore been placed on all He said and did in the Father's name.

He is gone to the Father; and it is clear therefore that He has been accepted as the Savior and Redeemer of men.

He is gone to the Father in the likeness and nature of men; evidently, then, man is an object of God's love, is reconciled to God, and is admitted to the rights and privileges of a son and heir.

The work of Jesus on man's behalf, finished at the cross, accepted by the Father—of which the resurrection is witness—presented by our Great High Priest within the veil, is the momentous truth which the Holy Spirit brings home to the convinced sinner. And inasmuch as we are unable to see within the veil and discern the divine marks of approval and acceptance, the Holy Spirit descends, and His advent proves that Jesus has gone where He said He would go, and has done what He promised.

How do we know that the work of Jesus Christ has been accepted in the courts of eternity? Because before He died the Master said that He was going to the Father, and that when He was glorified He would ask and receive the Spirit in His fullness. After days had elapsed and the second week from His ascension was already passing, the Spirit in pentecostal fullness fell on the waiting church, giving it an altogether new power with which to combat the world. What the carts of food were to Jacob, proving that Joseph lived and thought of him still, and was indeed supreme in Egypt, that the day of Pentecost was in declaring that Christ's personal righteousness had been vindicated, and that the righteousness He had wrought out for man had received the hallmark of the divine approval. Therefore the apostle says, "The Holy Ghost also is a witness to us that he hath perfected for ever by one offering them that are sanctified." And again, "Him hath God exalted with his right hand to be a Prince and a Saviour; and the Holy Ghost, whom God hath given to them that obey him, is witness of these things."

**The Conviction of Judgment**

When we have been freed *from* sin, and made righteous in Christ, we are left face to face with a tremendous struggle *against* sin. The sin of the past is indeed forgiven, the voice of conscience has been hushed, the sinner rejoices to know that he is accepted on the ground of righteousness; but the old temptations still crop up. Passion prompts us to live for present gratification; the flesh deadens the burning aspirations of the spirit. We ask in sad earnestness, "How shall we be able to survive the terrible struggle and come off victorious?" It appears a vain hope that we should ever rise to perfect and victorious purity.

At such a time the Comforter convinces us of judgment. Not, as the words are so often misquoted, of judgment *to come*; but in the sense in which our Lord spoke of judgment to the inquiring Greeks: "Now is the judgment of this world; now shall the prince of this world be cast out" (John 12:31). Our Lord's references to the existence and power of Satan are always distinct and unhesitating. It is impossible to accept Him as our supreme Teacher without accepting His statements concerning His great antagonist, to undo whose work brought the Son of God to earth.

The whole gospel is a story of the duel in which our Lord forever worsted and mastered Satan. The conflict began with the lonely struggle of the temptation in the wilderness; it pervaded Christ's earthly career; it culminated in the cross. Its first note was, "If thou be the Son of God, command that these stones be made bread" (Matt. 4:3); its last note was, "If thou be the son of God, come down from the cross" (Matt. 27:40). But when our Lord cried, "It is finished!" with the shout of a conqueror He proclaimed to the universe that, though tempted to the uttermost, He had not yielded in one particular, that evil was not an eternal power, that wrong was not omnipotent. The cross was the crisis of this world's history: the prince of this world measured himself for one final wrestle with the Son of God. Had he succeeded, evil would have reigned; but since he failed, he fell as lightning from heaven.

On this fact the Holy Spirit loves to dwell. He unfolds its full meaning. "See," He says, "Christ has conquered for you, and in your nature. You meet a foe who is not invincible. Christ conquered, not for Himself, but for all who believe. The prince of this world has been judged and found wanting. He is condemned for evermore. Only abide in the last Adam, the Lord from heaven, and let Him abide in you, and He will repeat through you His old victories."

What a majestic thought is here! The world comes to us first with her fascinations and delights. She comes to us next with her frowns and tortures. Behind her is her prince. But since he has been cast out by a Stronger than himself, and exists only on sufferance, his most potent bribes and lures, his most violent onsets, his most unscrupulous suggestions must collapse. Believer, meet him as a discredited and fallen foe. He can have no power at all over you. The cross bruised his head. You have no need to fear judgment. It awaits only those who are still in the devil's power. But you may rejoice that for you a victory waits, the measure of which will only be realized when you see the devil cast into the bottomless pit, and from there into the lake of fire.

# 19 Christ's Reticence Supplemented by the Spirit's Advent

*I have yet many things to say unto you; but ye cannot bear them now.*

*John 16:12*

How confidently our Lord speaks of the Spirit's advent; not more so did the prophets foretell His own. Repeatedly He returns to the phrase, *When He is come.* The advent of the Spirit to the heart of the church on the day of Pentecost was as distinct and marked an event as the advent of the Son of God Himself to the manger bed of Bethlehem. Let every reader of these words be sure to take full advantage of the presence of the Spirit, just as we would wish to have availed ourselves to the uttermost of the physical presence of Christ, had our lot so befallen.

**The Theme of This Paragraph Is the Incompleteness of Our Lord's Teaching**

For three and a half years He was perpetually pouring forth His wonderful words; in many *different* places—the marketplace, the home at Bethany, the hillside, the temple cloister; to many *different audiences*—now in thronging crowds, and again to the secret disciple whose footfall startled the night, or the lone woman drawing water from the well; on many *different themes*—to mention all of which would be impossible, thought He never spoke on any subject, common as a wayside flower, without associating with it thoughts that can never die. We have but a small portion of His words recorded in the Gospels; it is therefore the more remarkable that He left anything unsaid, and that at the close of His ministry He should have to say, *I have yet many things to say unto you.* Many parables, fair as His tenderest, woven in the productive loom of His imagination, remained unuttered; many discourses, inimitable as the Sermon on the Mount, or as this in the Upper Room, unspoken; many heavenly mysteries unrevealed.

A comparison between the Gospels and the Epistles will indicate how much our Lord had left unsaid. The relation of the law of Moses to His finished work was left to the Epistle to the Romans: the relation between His church and the usages of the heathen world, for the Epistle to Corinth: the effect of His resurrection on the sleeping saints, for the Epistle to the Thessalonians. He said nothing about the union of Jew and Gentile on terms of equality in His church; this mystery, hidden from ages and from generations, was only fully unveiled in the Epistle to the Ephesians. It was left for the Epistle to the Hebrews to disclose the superseding of the temple and its ritual by the realities of the Christian dispensation. The practical precepts for the right ordering of the churches were left for the Pastoral Epistles; and the course of the church through the ages of the world's history, for the Apocalypse of the beloved apostle. When we perceive the many things, taught in the Epistles, which were not unfolded by the Lord, we discern a fresh meaning in His assurance that He left much unsaid.

We are perpetually assailed by the cry, "Back to Christ," which is significant of men's weariness of theological system and organized ecclesiasticism, and of a desire to get away from the accretions of the Middle Ages and the dead hand of church tradition, into the pure, serene, and holy presence of Jesus of Nazareth. It always seems to us as if the cry should be *Up* to Christ, rather than *Back* to Him. To put it as men generally do, suggests the inference that Christ lies far in the wake of human progress, and behind the haze of eighteen centuries; that He was, but is no longer, a potent factor in the world's life: whereas He is here, now, with us, in us, leading us as of old through rugged passes, and to mountains of transfiguration.

If the endeavor to get back to Christ means the reception of the synoptic Gospels to the exclusion of the fourth, or the

Epistles; or the Sermon on the Mount to the exclusion of the Epistle to the Romans; or Jesus to the exclusion of His apostles—we feel it is but half the truth. Our Lord Himself protested that His teachings were incomplete; that there was much left unsaid that would be said by the Comforter, as even He could not—because the Spirit of God speaks in the inner shrine of the soul, uttering to the inner ear truths which no voice could speak or ear receive. Let us always remember therefore that the Gospels must be completed by the Epistles; and that the Spirit who spake in the Son spake also in those whom the Son had prepared to be His mouthpieces to men.

**The Partial Measure of Human Ability to Know**

"Ye cannot bear them now." Our Lord's reticence did not arise from ignorance—all things were naked and open to His eye; but He had a tender regard for these men whom He loved.

*Their bodies* could not bear more. When the mind is strongly imposed on, the delicate organism of the body is deeply affected. On the banks of the river Hiddekel, words of such wondrous importance were uttered to Daniel, that the lonely exile fainted, and was sick many days. "When I saw Him," said John, "I fell at his feet as dead." Flavel, on more than one occasion, asked that the excessive revelation might be stayed. Our Lord, therefore, feared that in their weakened state, torn by anxiety and sorrow, His followers would collapse if further strain were imposed on their powers of spiritual apprehension.

*Their minds* could not bear more. The mind cannot receive more than a certain amount. After awhile its eye gets weary, it ceases to receive, and even to remember. There are multitudes of cases in which, when too great a weight has been crowded on the delicate organism through which thoughts move, its balance has been upset, and it has driveled into idiocy. Against this danger, also, our Lord guarded, for His disciples were already excited and overstrained. Their brains were so exhausted that in a few moments they would be sleeping on the cold ground of Gethsemane. Had He poured the light of the other world in full measure on them, the tide of glory had submerged them, like spent swimmers.

*Their affections* could not bear more. Because He had spoken to them, sorrow had filled their heart; and He forbore to describe the valley of the shadow through which they were still to pass, lest their hearts should break. They had hardly began to drink its cup: what would its dregs be? The footmen had wearied them: how would they contend with the horses? The brink had terrified them: how would they do in the swellings of Jordan?

It is thus that He deals with us still. He knows our frame, and proportions our trials to our strength. He carefully feels our pulse before beginning the operation through which He would lead us to perfect health. He tempers His discipline to our spiritual capacity. We desire to know many things: the reason why sin has been permitted; the fate of the impenitent; the state of the great masses of men who have passed into eternity without a true knowledge of God. Peter asks for John, "What shall this man do?" Each wants to know the secret plans, whether for himself, or his beloved, which are lying in the mind and purpose of the Eternal. What will the end be? Where does that path lead by which I am going, and which descends steeply into the ravine? Will the fight between evil and good be prolonged? What are hell, and the bottomless pit, and the meaning of Christ's references to the undying worm and unquenchable flame? And Christ says, "My child, you cannot bear it; you could not sleep at night, you could not play with the merry children by day, you could not perform your slender tasks, if you knew all that I know, and see as I see. Be at rest. Trust Me. I will tell you as soon as you are strong enough. Nothing will be kept back from you, all will be revealed." And surely the sufferings and limitations of this present time will not be worthy to be compared with the exceeding weight of glory, when in the presence of our Lord we shall see eye to eye, and know even as we are known.

In the light of these words we may get comfort. When some crushing trouble befalls us, He who only spoke as they were able to bear will not permit the flame to be hotter, the tide stronger, or the task more trying, than we have strength for. We often do not know our strengh nor the power of His grace. Sorrow may be sent to reveal us to ourselves, and show how much spiritual energy we have been silently acquiring. Do not therefore run to and fro and say, "It is too much, I cannot bear it." But know and be sure that Christ has ascertained your resources, and is sure of your ability, before He permits the extreme ordeal to overtake you. Dare to say with the apostle, "I can do all things through Christ who strengtheneth me" (Phil. 4:13).

**The Teaching of the Divine Spirit**

His *personality* is unmistakable; though the Greek word for Spirit is neuter, a masculine pronoun is used in conjunction with it when Jesus says, "He, the Spirit of truth." The personal Christ sent as a substitute for Himself no mere breath or influence, but the personal Spirit. The Advocate before the throne is well represented by the Advocate in the heart of the church; and these two agree in one—distinct as different persons, but one in the mystical unity of the Holy Trinity.

Note the *method* of the Holy Spirit. He teaches truth by taking of the things of Christ and revealing them. There are two methods of teaching children—by precept, and by example. I go into a schoolroom one summer afternoon, and notice the hot cheeks and tired eyes of the little ones. Outside the open window the bees are droning past, the butterflies flit from flower to flower, and nature seems to cry to the little hearts, "Come and play with me." Does a garden ever look so beautiful as to children shut up to their studies? "What are you learning, little ones?" I say. "Botany," is the sad answer. "We've got to learn all these hard names, and copy these diagrams." "Well," I say, "shut up your books, and come with me." And presently I teach them more botany by contact with the flowers themselves, than they would have learned by hours of poring over lesson books. It is so the Spirit teaches. Is gentleness or purity, self-sacrifice or prayer, the lesson that we are set to acquire? There is no need for Him to make a new revelation to us. It is enough if He but bring us face to face with Jesus, and show these qualities shining through his words and deeds. The truth certainly, but the truth as it is in Jesus.

The condition of proficiency in the Spirit's school is *obe-*

*dience.* "He will *guide* you into all truth." This word is very significant. Literally it means, *Show the way.* Ordinarily, men ask to know the truth before they obey. The Spirit demands that they should obey before they know. Let me know the outcome of this act—its philosophy, its reasonableness, its result—then I will obey. But the Spirit answers, "It is enough for you, O child of man, to know Me. Can you not trust? Will you not obey? And as you obey you shall know. Take this path, plod along its difficult way, climb where it climbs; so shall you ascend the steep of obedience, and at each step a further horizon of the truth will open spread out beneath you."

Let us be more sensitive to the guidance of the Spirit, following wherever He clearly indicates—as when the Spirit said to Philip, "Go, join thyself to this chariot." We shall know when we follow on to know the Lord. His going forth is prepared for those who are prepared to obey whatever He may appoint.

The *purpose* of the Spirit is to glorify our Lord. "He shall glorify me, for he shall receive of mine." The Spirit's presence, as such, should not be a subject of our close scrutiny, lest we conflict with His holy purpose of being hidden, that Jesus may be all in all before the gaze of saint and sinner. He is so anxious that nothing should divert the soul's gaze from the Lord whom He would reveal, that He carefully withdraws Himself from view. "There must be nothing, not even God Himself, to distract the heart from Jesus, through whom we come to God. But remember that when you have the most precious views of your dear Lord, it is because the Holy Spirit, all unseen, is witnessing and working within you."

The *authority* of the Holy Spirit appears in the words, "He shall not speak of himself; but whatsoever he shall hear, that shall he speak." Where does He hear the truths He utters? Where? There is only one place. In the depths of the eternal throne, in the heart of Deity itself, in the secret place of the Most High. Oh, marvel! surpassing thought, yet true—that things which pass between the Father and the Son, in the depths which no angel can penetrate, may be disclosed and made known to those humble and contrite hearts who are willing to make a space and pause for the divine Spirit to speak the deep things of God.

May it be ours to be patient and willing pupils in this heavenly school, in which the Holy Spirit is Teacher, and Jesus the Textbook, and obedience the essential condition of knowledge.

# 20 The Conqueror of the World

*In the world ye shall have tribulation: but be of good cheer; I have overcome the world.*

*John 16:33*

It was the road between Jerusalem and the Gate of the Garden. Behind, lay the city bathed in slumber; before, the Mount of Olives with its terraced gardens; above, the Passover moon, pouring down floods of silver light that dropped to the ground through the waving branches of the trees. The Lord was on His way to betrayal and death, along that path flecked by checkered moonlight.

The farewell talk had been prolonged until the disciples had grasped something of the Master's meaning. With many a comforting assurance it had borne them forward to the magnificent but simple declaration, "I came forth from the Father, and am come into the world; again, I leave the world, and go to the Father" (v. 28). At that announcement light seems to have broken in upon their hearts, and they said to Him, "Lo, now speakest thou plainly: . . . by this we believe that thou camest forth from God." Jesus replied—not as translators render it, "Do ye now believe?" but as it should be rendered, "At last ye believe": and He proceeded to formulate three paradoxes:

First, that within an hour or so He would be alone, yet not alone.

Second, that they would have tribulation, and yet be in peace.

Third, that though He was going to His death, He was certainly a Conqueror, and had overcome the world, whose princes were about to crucify Him.

The word "overcome" occurs but twice in the recorded sayings of our Lord; in the present instance it made a lasting impression on the apostle John, who constantly makes use of it in his Epistles. We meet with it six times in his First Epistle, and sixteen times in the Book of Revelation. Who can forget the sevenfold promise spoken by the risen Lord to those who overcome; or the sublime affirmation concerning the martyrs, that they overcame by the blood of the Lamb and by the word of their testimony?

**Christ and His Disciples have a Common Foe**

"The world." And what is the world? It is good to take the inspired definition given in 1 John 2:16. After enumerating her three daughters—the lust of the flesh, the lust of the eyes, and the pride of life—the apostle goes on to say: "All that is in the world . . . is not of the Father," i.e. does not orginate or proceed from Him, but has its source in the world itself. We might reverse this proposition and say: "All that does not emanate from the Father, which you cannot trace back to His purpose in creation, is that mysterious indefinable influence or spirit that makes the world." The world, in this sense, is not primarily a thing, or a collection of people, but a spiritual influence poured out into the very atmosphere of our lives.

The spirit of the world insinutates itself everywhere. It is what we call society; the consensus of fashionable opinion; the spirit that finds its satisfaction in the seen and transient; the ambition that is encircled by the rim of an earthly horizon; the aims, plans, and activities, which are comprehended, as the Preacher says, "under the sun." You meet it in the school, where little children judge each other by their dress and the number of cars their fathers have; in the city, where strict lines are drawn between the professional or wholesale man and the retailer; in gatherings of well-dressed people, stiff with decorum and the punctilious observance of etiquette.

The world has formulated its *beatitudes*, thus:

"Blessed are the rich: for they shall inherit the earth."

"Blessed are the light-hearted: for they shall have many friends."

"Blessed are the respectable: for they shall be respected."

"Blessed are they who are not troubled by a sensitive conscience: for they shall succeed in life."

"Blessed are they who can indulge their appetites to the full: for they shall be filled."

"Blessed are they who have no need to conciliate their rivals: for they will be saved from anxiety."

"Blessed are they who have no poor relatives: for they shall be delivered from annoyance."

"Blessed are they of whom all men speak well."

The world's code says, "Do as others do; don't be singular; never offend against good taste; have a tinge of religiousness, but remember that too much is impracticable for daily life; whatever you do, don't be poor; never yield an inch, unless you are going to make something by the concession; take every advantage of bettering your position, it matters not at what cost to others—they must look after themselves, as you to yourself."

But it was reserved for John Bunyan to draw Madame Bubble's portrait: "This woman is a witch. 'I am mistress of the world,' she says, 'and men are made happy by me.' She wears a great purse at her side; and her hand is often in her purse fingering her money. Yea, she has bought off many a man from a pilgrim's life after he had fairly begun it. She is a bold and impudent slut also, for she will talk to any man. If there be one cunning to make money, she will speak well of him from house to house. None can tell of the mischief she does. She makes variance betwixt rulers and subjects, 'twixt parents and children, 'twixt a man and his wife, 'twixt the flesh and the heart. 'Had she stood by all this while,' said Standfast, whose eyes were still full of her, 'you could not have set Madame Bubble more amply before me, nor have better described her features.' 'He that drew her picture was a good limner,' said Mr. Honest, 'and he that so wrote of her said true.' 'Oh,' said Standfast, 'what a mercy it is that I did resist her! for to what might she not have drawn me.!' "

**Christ and His Disciples Have a Common Conflict**

It is inevitable that there should be collision, and therefore conflict, and as a result tribulation. The world spirit will not brook our disagreement with its plans and aims; and therefore they who persist in living godly lives in this present evil world must suffer persecution.

*Conflict about the use of power and prerogative.* At His baptism our Lord was proclaimed to be the Son of the Highest, and anointed with the Holy Spirit and with power. Instantly the prince of this world came to Him with the suggestion that He should use it for the purposes of His own comfort and display. "Make these stones bread for Your hunger; cast Yourself down and attract the attention of the crowds." Here were the lust of the flesh and the lust of the eyes. But our Lord refused to use for Himself the power that was entrusted to Him for the benediction and help of men.

*Conflict as to the way of helping and saving men.* The world's way was to leap into the seat of power at any cost, and from the height of universal authority administer the affairs of the world. But Christ knew better. He saw that He must take the form of a servant, and humble Himself to the lowest. If He would save men, He could not save Himself: if He would bring forth much fruit, He had to fall into the ground to die: if He would ascend far above all heavens, bearing us with Him to the realms of eternal day, He had to descend first into the lower parts of the earth.

*Conflict in the estimate of poverty and suffering.* The world looked on these as the most terrible disasters that could befall. Christ, on the other hand, taught that blessedness lay most within reach of the poor in spirit, the mourners, the merciful, the forgiving, and the persecuted. But the Pharisees, who were lovers of money, when they heard all these things, scoffed at Him.

*Conflict in their diverse notions of royalty.* The Jews looked for a Messiah who should revive the glories of the days of David and Solomon, driving the Gentiles from the land, and receiving the homage of the surrounding nations, while every son of Abraham enjoyed opulence and ease. Referring to this expectation, the Master said, "My kingdom is not of this world:

if my kingdom were of this world, then would my servants fight" (John 18:36). His conception of royalty was founded on service, which would wash the disciples' feet; on humility, which meekly bore the heavy yoke; on patience, which would not quench the smoking flax; on suffering, which flinched not from the cross; on the nobility and dignity of the inner life, which shone through the most humble circumstances, as the transfiguration glory through His robes. For this He died. The chief priests and scribes hunted Him to death, because He persisted in asserting that He was the true King of men. "And Pilate wrote a title, and put it on the cross, *Jesus of Nazareth, the King of the Jews*" (John 19:19).

*Conflict in regard to religion.* The people of Christ's day were very religious. The world likes a flavor of religion. It makes a good background and screen; it serves to hide much that is unbecoming and questionable; it is respectable, and satisfies an instinctive longing of the soul. The world, however, manages its religion in such a way as not to interfere with its self-aggrandizement, but, in fact, to promote it. Christ, on the other hand, taught that religion was for the Father in secret; and consisted not in the rigorous observance of outward rite, but in pity, mercy, forgiveness, solitary prayer, and purity of heart.

Thus the Lord's life was the reversal of everything that the world prized. Wherever He touched it there was conflict and collision, strong antagonism was evoked, and profound irritation on the part of the poor hollow appearance-loving world. So it must be with His followers. "These pilgrims must needs go through the fair. Well, so they did; but behold, even as they entered into the fair, all the people in the fair were moved, and the town itself as it were in a hubbub about them. They were clothed with such kind of raiment as was diverse from the raiment of any who traded in that fair; few could understand what they said; and the pilgrims set very light by all their wares. And they did not believe them to be any other than bedlams and mad. Therefore they took them and beat them, and besmeared them with dirt, and then put them in the cage, that they might be made a spectacle to all the men at the fair."

Child of God, your conflict may be altogether hidden from the eyes of those around you, lonely with the awful loneliness of one in a crowd of unsympathizing strangers, painful with the tribulation that Christ foretold. You have been ridiculed, sneered at, maligned; your tools hidden, your goods injured, violence threatened or executed. You have been as a speckled bird, pecked at by the birds around. But this is the way the Master went. By these marks you may be sure that you are in the way of His steps.

**The Common Victory**

"Be of good cheer; I have overcome the world."

In the midst of a battle, when the soldiers are weary with fatigue, galled with fire, and grimed with smoke, if the general rides into the midst to cheer them with a few hearty words, and tells them that the key to the position is in their hands, they cheer him enthusiastically, and take up new hope. So down the line our Leader and Commander sends the encouragement of these inspiring words. Let us drink their comfort and encouragement to the full, that, amid our tribulation, in Him we may have peace.

*He conquered for Himself.* The Lord has shown that a great and blessed life is possible on conditions that the world pronounces simply unendurable. He would not accept the world's maxims, would not be ruled by the world's principles, did despite to the world's most favorite plans. He even tasted the dregs of reprobation that the world metes out to those who oppose her, enduring the cross, and despising the shame. But His life was blessed while it lasted; His name is the dearest and fairest treasure of our race; and He holds an empire such as none of the world's most favored conquerors ever won. Does not this show that the world is a lying temptress; that there is another and a better policy of life than hers; that the real sweets and prizes of this brief existence are, after all, not in her gift? Christ has overcome the world. Her prince came to Him, but found no response to any of His proposals. He disregarded her flatteries and threatenings; He would not have her help and despised her hate; He prosecuted His path in defiance of her, and has left an imperishable glory behind. Thus He overcame the world.

*And He conquered as our Representative and Head.* What He did for Himself He is prepared to repeat in the life story of His followers. Ah! lonely soul, you shall not be left unaided to withstand the seductions of the temptress world; Jesus is with you, your Great-heart and Champion. As the Father was with Him, so He is with you; so thus you may boldly say, "The Lord is my helper: I will not fear what man shall do unto me" (Heb. 13:6).

He does more. Behind the light of this world's glory, Jesus reveals another; and it is as when the sun rises, while the yellow moon still lingers in the sky. She comes to have no glory by reason of that glory that excells. We are content with this world until He reveals the glory of the unseen and eternal; then a holy discontent arises within us, such as the patriarchs felt toward Canaan, when by faith they beheld the city that has foundations. I only say to you, get that vision, and it becomes as easy for you to refuse the passing and worthless attractions of the world as for an angel to ignore a wanton's beauty, or a child to make light of diamonds in the rough.

In Jesus you may have peace. It is not certainly ours, unless we follow the two conditions He lays down. First, of abiding in Him; and, second, of meditating on His words. But if these be observed, we shall have peace in the midst of strife, just as there is an oratory in the heart of the castle tower; a hollow cone in the midst of the candle flame; and a center of safety in the midst of the sweeping whirlwind. Oh, abide there, child of God!

And, in addition to peace, there shall one day be victory. We also shall overcome, and shall sit with Christ on His throne, as He overcame, and sits with the Father on His. Then the fruit of the tree of life, immunity from the second death, the hidden manna, the white stone, the morning star, the confession before the angels of God, and the pillar in the temple of eternity!

# 21 Consecrated to Consecrate

*For their sakes I sanctify myself that they themselves also may be sanctified in truth*

*John 17:19* (RV)

"The most precious fragment of the past," is the unstinted eulogium that a thoughtful man has passed on this transcendent prayer; transcending in its scope of view, its expressions, its tender pathos, all other prayers of which we have record.

Its primary characteristic is *timelessness.* Though uttered within a few hours of Calvary, it contains thoughts and expressions that must have been familiar to our Lord at any moment during the centuries that have followed. As we study it, therefore, we are listening to words that have been uttered many times on our behalf, and will be uttered until we are with Him, where He is, beholding the glory of the divine Son, superadded to that of the perfect Servant.

The margin substitutes the word "consecrate" for "sanctify"; and it probably conveys a better meaning, because devotion to the will of God is prominent, rather than the holiness of personal character. Devotion to God's will is the primary thought suggested by the word; but of course it involves a blameless and spotless character. Thus we might read the words, "For their sakes I consecrate Myself, that they also may be consecrated in truth." Through the dim twilight the Lord clearly foresaw what was awaiting Him—the agony and bloody sweat, the cross and passion, the forsakenness and travail of His soul. The cross with outstretched arms waited to receive Him; the midnight darkness to engulf Him; the murderous band to wreak their hate on the unresisting Lamb—and yet He did not flinch, but went right forward, consecrating Himself.

> Twas thus He suffered, though a Son,
> Foreknowing, choosing, tasting all;
> Until the dreadful work was done,
> And drank the bitter cup of gall.

**The Subjects of Christ's Solicitude**

In earlier verses the Lord speaks of Himself, of His finished work, of the glory that He had left, of that to which He went; asking only that He might be able to glorify the Father in every movement of His coming sorrow (vv. 1-5).

Then he launches Himself on the full current of intercession, and pleads for those who had been given to Him, as distinguished from the world of men out of which they had come. Evidently the same thought was in His mind as inspired His words in John 10, when He spoke of the sheep whom the Father had given to Him, that he might give them eternal life (vv. 27-29). And it may be that each of these two utterances was inspired by older words yet, that Zechariah had addressed to the poor of the flock when he cut in two his two staffs, Beauty and Bands (Zech. 11:7-14).

The underlying conception in all these passages seems to be that the Father has entrusted to the special keeping of Jesus certain elect spirits having an affinity to His nature, and who should stand in the inner circle to Him because they have been associated with Him from high redemptive purpose. All souls are God's by right of creation, and all are included in the redemption wrought on the cross; but not all had been included in the divine gift of which Jesus speaks, "Thine they were, and thou gavest them me" (John 17:6). We conclude that in the eternity of the past, as the Father beheld all future things as though they were present, and surveyed the vast multitudes of the human family, He discerned those who would be attracted by indissoluble union with His Son manifest in the flesh; and whom He did foreknow, these also He did predestinate to be His flock, His brothers and sisters,

His chosen band of associates in His redemptive purpose. These were the subjects of His powerful solicitude, "I make request, not for the world, but for those whom thou has given me" (John 17:9).

What then? Did not God care for the world? Certainly. He so loved the world that He gave His only begotten Son.

How then can we reconcile the love of God to the world with the selection of some as the flock of the Lamb, while the great world seems expressly excluded from His prayer? That question is fitly put. The emphasis is on the word "seems." It is only to the superficial view that the world is excluded. Are the planets excluded from the law of gravitation because suns are filled with fire and light? Are the lower orders of creation excluded from the circle of enjoyment because man with His high organization is more richly endowed than they? Are sufferers excluded from the healing virtues of nature because a comparative few are especially qualified as surgeons and physicians? Can a missionary be charged with neglecting a dark continent because he concentrates thought and care on a few elect spirits gathered around him? For instance, could Columba be held guilty of neglecting the Picts and Scots when on Iona's lone isle he focused his care on the handful of followers who assembled around the ancient pile, whose ruins are his lasting memorial? There is but one answer to these questions. Election is not exclusive, but inclusive. Its purpose is not primarily the salvation or delectation of the few; but their equipment to become the apostles to the many. And if Jesus thought, cared, and prayed so much for those whom the Father had given Him, His ulterior thought was that the world might believe that the Father had sent Him (v. 21). If, then, it should be proved that you, my reader, are not included in the band of the given ones, that would not necessarily involve you in the eternal condemnation and loss of the future; though it would exclude you from sharing with Christ in His lofty mission to the sons of men.

What are the marks, then, that we belong to the inner circle of the given ones? They are these—

1. That we have come to Him (John 6:37).

2. That we hear His voice, listening for the slightest indication of His will (John 10:27).

3. That we follow His steps through the world.

4. That we receive His words and believe that the Father sent the Son to be our Savior.

5. That the world hates us (v. 14).

Wherever these marks are present, they indicate the hand of the Great Shepherd and Bishop of souls; and though we be among the most timid and worthless of the flock, He is pledged to keep us so that none shall snatch us from His hand, and to conduct us through the valley of the shadow to those dewy upland lawns over which He will lead us for evermore.

**What He Sought for Them**

"That they might be consecrated in truth."

Christ does not ask that His own should be forgiven, comforted, supplied with the good things of life—all thought for these pales in the presence of His intense desire that they should be consecrated, that is, inspired by the same consuming passion as was burning in His heart. He knew that He was no more in the world. High business connected with its interests summoned Him to the far country, where He went to receive the kingdom and return. But He desired that the passion that filled His soul, His tears, His prayers, and, to some degree, His sufferings, might always be represented among the sons of men, might be embodied in human lives, might find utterance through human lips. He could not Himself perpetuate His corporeal, visible ministry among men; and therefore desired with a great desire that those whom the Father had given Him should evermore "show the Lord's death till he come"—not simply by gathering at His table, but by going forth to live His life, and to fill up that which is behind of His sufferings.

Is this your life? We have sometimes heard consecration stated as though it were a matter of choice whether believers should bind themselves by its obligations or not. When a student enters the university there are certain subjects in which he must matriculate, but there are special ones that he may graduate in or not, as he pleases. Should he refuse them, he is not blamed. The matter is within his option. Now, let it be clearly understood from these words of Christ that consecration is not in the same sense optional, but obligatory. For all those whom the Father had given Him He pleaded with His dying breath that they should be consecrated; and if you are not consecrated—if there are extensive reserves in your life, if you are holding back part of the price, if you are saying of anything that you have, "It is my own, I shall do as I choose"—then understand that you are in direct conflict with Christ's purpose and prayer. He asked that you might be consecrated; and you have chosen to regard consecration as the craze of the fervid enthusiast.

**Christ's Method of Securing the Consecration of His Servants**

"For their sakes I consecrate myself."

*There is the potency of example.* "Leaving us an example, that ye should follow his steps" (1 Peter 2:21). "He that saith he abideth in him ought himself also so to walk, even as he walked" (1 John 2:6). Once when He was praying in a certain place His disciples said, "Lord, teach us to pray." They had come within the powerful attraction of His Spirit. Like a swift current it had caught them, and they were eager to emulate Him. It is impossible for the saint to gaze long on the *stigmata* without becoming branded with the marks of Jesus; impossible to see Him hastening to the cross without being stirred to follow Him; impossible to behold the intensity of His purpose for a world's redemption without becoming imbued with it; impossible to see Him in love with the cross without feeling a similar infatuation. And it is impossible to behold Him plunging into the dark floods of death that He might emerge in the sunlit ocean, without the consciousness of the uprising of an insatiable desire to be like Him, to drink of His cup, and be baptized with His baptism, to fall into the ground to die that He may not abide alone, to know the fellowship of His sufferings and conformity to His death, that He may appoint unto us a kingdom, as the Father has appointed to Him.

*There is our implication in his mediatorial work.* "I am

crucified with Christ," the apostle said (Gal. 2:20). And again, "Ye died with Christ from the rudiments of the world" (Col. 2:20). Of course, Christ died *for* us, presenting to the claims of a broken law a perfect satisfaction and oblation. It is also true that we died *with* Him, were *in* Him as our Representative, wrought *through* Him as our Forerunner; the first-fruit sheaf contained the promise of all its companions.

Consider for a moment a remarkable expression that casts light on this whole subject. In that memorable discussion with the Jews in Solomon's porch, which practically closed our Lord's public ministry, He said that the Father had sanctified and consecrated Him and sent Him into the world (John 10:36). In these sublime words He undoubtedly refers to a moment that preceded the Incarnation, when the Godhead designated the Second Person to redeem men. Was it the same moment, think you, as that in which Jesus said, "Sacrifice and offering thou wouldest not, but a body thou hast prepared me (or, mine ears hast thou pierced). I delight to do thy will, O my God"? (Ps. 40:6, 8). If so, what an august scene that must have been when, in the presence of the assembled hierarchies of heaven, the Father solemnly set apart the Son for His redemption work; consecrating Him to bring in everlasting salvation, to destroy the works of the devil, and to bring together in one the children of God that are scattered abroad!

In that solemn consecration of the Head all the members were included. The King stood for His kingdom; the Shepherd for His flock. Any who refuse to be consecrated contravene and contradict that momentous decision.

When Christ approached His death in these words, He renewed His act of consecration, and again implicated those who belong to Him; bearing us with Him, He went to the cross; involving us by His actions, He yielded Himself up to death. In His holy purpose we were quickened together with Him, and raised up together, and made to sit altogether in the heavenly places; and by the same emphasis with which we declare ourselves to be His, we confess that we are among those who are bound to a life of consecration. We are pledged to it by union with our Lord. We cannot draw back from the doorpost to which He was nailed without proving that we are deficient in appreciating the purpose that brought Him to our world, the surrender that withheld not His face from spitting, His soul from the shadow of death.

**Our Duty** "Yield yourselves unto God" (Rom. 6:13). When Abraham Lincoln dedicated, for the purposes of a graveyard, the field of Gettysburg, where so many brave soldiers had lost their lives, he said: "We cannot dedicate, we cannot consecrate, we cannot hallow this ground. The brave men who struggled here have consecrated it far beyond our power to add or detract. It is for us, the living, rather to be dedicated to the unfinished work which they who fought here have thus far so nobly advanced. It is rather for us to be here dedicated to the great task remaining before us, that from these honored dead we take increased devotion to that cause for which they gave the last full measure of devotion; and that we here highly resolve that these dead shall not have died in vain."

These noble words, when we have made the needful alterations and adaptations, are most applicable to our present point. Let us dedicate ourselves to the great task before us, and to which Jesus has pledged us. Let us devote ourselves to the great cause for which Jesus died. Let us highly resolve that He shall not have died in vain. Let us offer and present ourselves, our souls and bodies, to be a reasonable, holy, and living sacrifice to God, that His will might be done through us, as it is done in heaven.

My Master, lead me to thy door;
Pierce this now willing ear once more;
Thy bonds are freedom, let me stay
With Thee, to toil, endure, obey.

Yes; ear and hand, and thought and will!
Use all in thy dear slavery still!
Self's weary liberties I cast
Beneath thy feet; there keep them fast.

# 22 The Lord's Prayer for His People's Oneness

*That they all may be one . . . one in us. . . . That they may be one, even as we are one . . . perfect in one.*

*John 17:21-23*

Thus our High Priest pleaded, and thus He pleads. In all the power of His endless life He ever lives to bear this great petition on His heart: and as the weight of the jeweled breastplate lay heavy on the heart of the high priest of old, so does it press on Him, as the ages slowly pass by in their never-ceasing progress toward the consummation of all things. Listen to that voice, sweet and full as the distant rush of many waters, as it pleads in the midst of eternity that those who believe in Him may be one.

Nor is it true that this prayer awaits an answer indefinitely future. There seems good reason to believe, as we shall see, that in these words our Lord was making a request that began to be fulfilled on the Day of Pentecost, and is being fulfilled continually—although the oneness that is being realized is still, like His kingdom, in mystery, and is waiting for the manifestation of the sons of God. Then, as the gauzy mists of time part before the breath of God, the accomplished oneness of the church shall stand revealed.

**The Oneness of Believers Is a Spiritual Oneness**

Can there be any reasonable doubt of this when our Master asks so clearly that we may be one, *as the Father and He are one*? The model for Christian unity is evidently the unity between the Father and Son by the Holy Spirit; and since that unity, the unity of the blessed

God, is not corporeal, nor physical, nor substantial to the eye of the flesh, may we not infer—no, are we not compelled to infer—that the oneness of believers is to be after the same fashion; and to consist in so close an identity of nature, so absolute an interfusion of spirit, as that they shall be one in aim, and thought, and life, and spirit—spiritually one with each other, because spiritually one with Him?

The Church of Rome, which has erred in gross material forms the most spiritual conceptions of God, sought to prove herself the true church by achieving a oneness of her own. It was an outward and visible oneness. In this church in the past everyone had to utter the same formularies, worship in the same postures, and belong to the same ecclesiastical system. And her leaders did their best to realize their dream. They endeavored to exterminate heresy by fire, and sword, and torture. They spread their network through the world. And just before the dawn of the Reformation they seemed to have succeeded. At the beginning of the sixteenth century, Europe reposed in the monotony of almost universal uniformity, beneath the almost universal supremacy of the papacy. Rome might indeed have adopted the insolent language of the Assyrian of prophecy: "As one gathereth eggs that are left, have I gathered all the earth; and there was none that moved the wing, or opened the mouth, or peeped." And what was the result? *What but the deep sleep of spiritual death.*

Many modern notions of Christian unity seem to proceed on the same line. The assent to a certain credal basis, the meeting in great catholic conventions, the exchange of pulpits—these seem to exhaust the conceptions of large numbers, and to satisfy their ideal. But surely there is a bond of union—deeper, holier, more vital and more blessed than any of these—that shyly reveals itself, now and again, in one or more of them, but is independent of all, and when all of them are wanting, still constitutes us *one*. And what is that bond of union but the possession of a common spiritual life, like that which unites the Father and Son; and which pervades us also, making us one with each other, because we are already one with God?

You may not care to admit it; you may even be ignorant of

the full meaning of this marvelous fact; you may live an exclusive life, never going beyond the walls of some small conventicle, or the barriers of some strict ecclesiastical system; you may bear yourself impatiently and brusquely toward those who differ from you; you may even brand them with your anathema: but if they are one with God, by His gracious indwelling Spirit of Life, and if you are also one with Him, you positively cannot help being one with them. Your creed may differ, or your mode of worship, or your views about the church; but you cannot be otherwise than one with those who are one with God, in a union that is not material but spiritual.

**This Oneness Also Admits of Great Variety**

"One; as thou, Father, art in me, and I in thee." Now, of course, we all admit the unity of the Godhead. The first article of the Jew is also the first article of the Christian, that the Lord our God is one God, one in essence, one in purpose, one in action. The Son does nothing of Himself; the Father does nothing apart from the Son; the Holy Spirit proceeds from the Father and the Son. We cannot, as yet, understand this mystery; but with reverence we accept it as the primary basis of our faith.

But though God is One, there is evidently a variety of function in the ever-blessed Trinity. The Father decrees, the Son executes. The Father sends, the Son is sent. The Father works in creation, the Son in redemption and judgment. And the functions of both Father and Son differ from those of the Holy Spirit.

Since then, according to our Lord's request, the unity of the church is to resemble the unity of the Godhead, we may expect that it will not be physical, nor mechanical, nor a uniformity; but that it will be variety in unity—a unity of spirit and purpose, and yet a unity that admits of very diverse functions and operations. Diversities of gifts, but the same Spirit; differences of administrations, but the same Lord; diversities of operations, but the same God who works all in all.

*The very conception of unity involves variety.* You take me out into a piece of wasteland, and pointing to a heap of bricks, say, "There is a unity." I at once rebut your assertion; there is uniformity undoubtedly, but not unity. Unity requires that a variety of *different* things should be combined to form one structure and carry out one idea. A collection bricks is not a unity, but a house is. A snow atom is not a unity, but a snow crystal is. And when our Lord spoke of His disciples as one, He not only expected that there would be varieties among them, in character, mind, and ecclesiastical preference; but by the very choice of His words He meant us to infer that it would be so. The unity on which He set His heart was not a uniformity.

*But with variety there may be the truest unity.* There is variety in the human body—from eyelash to foot, from heart to blood cell, from brain to quivering nerve fiber; yet, in all this variety, each one is conscious of an indivisible unity. There is variety in the tree: the giant arms that wrestle with the storm, the far-spreading roots that moor it to the soil, the myriad leaves in which the wind makes music, the cones or nuts that it flings on the forest floor; yet for all this it is one. There is variety in the Bible: variety of authorship—king, prophet, priest, herdman, fisherman, scholar, sage, and saint; variety of style—prose, poetry, psalmody, argument, appeal; variety of age—from the days of Moses to those of John, the beloved apostle, writing amid the persecutions of the empire. Yet for all this there is a oneness in the Bible that no mere binding could give. So with the church of Christ: there may be, there must be, infinite varieties and shades of thought and work. Some will prefer the methods of Wesley, others the freedom of Congregationalism. Some will pray most naturally through the venerable words of a liturgy, others in the deep silence of a Friends' Meeting; some will thrive best beneath the crozier of the Bishop, others in the plain barracks of the Salvation Army. But, notwithstanding all this variety, there may be a deep spiritual unity—many folds, but one flock; many regiments, but one army; many stones, but one breastplate. "There is one body, and one Spirit, even as ye are called in one hope of your calling; one Lord, one faith, one baptism, one God and Father of all, who is above all, and through all, and in you all" (Eph. 4:4-6).

**The Basis of Christian Unity Is the Union of Each Believer to Christ**

"I in them . . . that they may be made perfect in one." However much true believers in Christ differ, there are two points in which they agree.

*Each believer is in Christ.* He is in Christ's heart, loved with an everlasting love, the beloved name engraven on its secret tables; in Christ's book, enrolled on those pages that are sealed so fast that He alone can break the sevenfold seal; in Christ's hand, which holds the ocean as a drop on its palm, and which was pierced on Calvary, from which no power shall ever pluck the trembling soul; in Christ's grace, rooted as a tree in luxuriant soil, or a house in a foundation of rock; but above all in Christ's Person, for He is the Head, "from whom the whole body is fitly framed and knit together by that which every joint supplieth" (Eph. 4:16). There are innumerable texts that speak of the church as the Body of Christ (Eph. 1:23; Col. 1:24); and as soon as a man believes in Christ, he becomes a member of that mystical body. "We are members of His body, of His flesh, and of His bones." You may be a very obscure member, or even a paralyzed member; but be sure of this, if you are a Christian you are in Christ, as the eye is in the eye socket, the arm in the shoulder joint, and the finger in the hand.

*Christ is in each believer.* The texts that teach Christ's real presence in the believer are as numerous as spring flowers. "Christ liveth in me" (Gal. 2:20). "Know ye not that Jesus Christ is in you, except ye be reprobates?" (2 Cor. 13:5). "Ye shall know that I am in my Father, and ye in me, and I in you." The Lord Jesus is in the heart that makes Him welcome—as the steam is in the piston, as the sap is in the branch, as the blood is in the heart, as the life is in the body. It would be impossible for words to describe a more intense spiritual Oneness that that which is here presented to us. The Savior is in each of us; as the Father is in Him and we are in Him, and He in God. "[Our] life is hid with Christ in God" (Col. 3:3). Therefore we are not only one with Jesus Christ, but through Him we are one with God. "I in them, thou in me." The very life of God is pouring its glorious tides through us, and would do so more if only we were more receptive and obedient. He pours water out of the mouth of the Congo at the rate of a million tons per second; and is willing to do marvels as mighty through each believer. And as this life permeates us all alike, it makes us one, not only with the blessed God, but with all who believe—as the blood makes all the members of the body one, and the sap the branches of the tree.

**The Means of This Spiritual Unity Are the Influences of the Holy Spirit.**

Influence means *inflow*. It was by the Holy Spirit that our Lord's human nature was made one with His Father's. And this same Holy Spirit He has bequeathed to us, that He may be the same bond of spiritual life between us and our Lord as He was between our Lord and His Father. May not this be the meeting of His words: "The glory which thou gavest me I have given them; that they may be one, even as we are one"? May not that glory have consisted in the oneness of His human nature with God the Father, by the Holy Spirit? And if so, it may be shared by us. The more believers receive the indwelling of the Holy Spirit, the more clearly will they appreciate this great mystery, and the more closely will they be drawn to all other believers; hushing jealous thoughts and uncharitable words, and "endeavoring to keep the unity of the Spirit in the bond of peace" (Eph. 3:3).

It is abundantly clear, then, that this unity cannot be broken unless we break away from Christ. Men have used the word "schism" with terrible effect. If a man has broken away from some visible church, they have pointed to him as schismatic. But what is schism? It is breaking away from the body of Christ. But what is the body of Christ? The Roman Catholic will tell you that it is the Church of Rome; the Anglican will tell you that it is the Church of England; the High Churchman will tell you that it is the collection of churches that hold the doctrine of Apostolical Succession. What vestige of scriptural proof is there for these assertions? What an absurdity it is to be told that we must submit to an outward rite, or we cannot belong to the body of Christ! What, then, would become of all the saints and martyrs who died without membership with one of these visible organizations? No; the body of Christ, as Scripture plainly teaches, is that great multitude that no man can number, of all nations, and kindreds, and peoples, and tongues, and sects, and eras, who are united by faith with the Savior. The church of Christ is not conterminous with any earthly or visible organization; it is long as the ages, wide as the poles, broad as the charity of God; it includes all in heaven and on earth who hold the Head. The only condition of membership in that church is simple faith in Christ. And the only method of severance from that church is through the severance of the soul's trust in Christ. He only is a schismatic who ceases to be Christ's.

The papal legate told Savonarola that he cut him off from the church militant and from the church triumphant. "From the Church Militant you may," was the martyr's reply; "but from the Church Triumphant, never!" It was well spoken; but Savonarola might have gone further, and defied the scarlet-coated functionary even to cut him off from the church militant—nothing could do that but apostasy. A man may be excommunicated from our church systems, or he may never have belonged to one of them; but so long as he believes in Christ, he is a member of the Holy Catholic Church. And schism is more likely to be charged against those who violate the spirit of Christian charity in making harsh and false statements against their fellow members in the body of Christ. Let us not retaliate, lest we also commit that sin. We can afford to wait. *Five minutes in heaven, or less, will settle it all.*

The object for which Christ prayed is already being partially accomplished. The world may not be as yet surrendering to the claims of Jesus Christ, but it is becoming increasingly impressed with His divine mission: "that the world may believe that thou hast sent me." And in proportion as the Holy Spirit pervades and fills the hearts of the children of God, the manifestation of the life of God in them and through them will have an ever-increasing effect, and will do what church systems and even the preachings of her thousand pulpits cannot effect in convincing and saving men.

Let us remember that Christ's own conception of the unity

of His church is that which is the result of the indwelling of the one Spirit. Such unity is already a fact in the eye of God, though undiscerned as yet in all its fullness by men. Let us thank God that this marvelous request has been already so largely realized; and let us dare to hold fellowship as Christians with all those who are indwelt by the Spirit of life which is also in Christ Jesus.